TRIPLE TESTED · FOR YOUR SUCCESS EVERY TIME ·

For more than 50 years, *The Australian Women's Weekly* Test Kitchen has been creating marvellous recipes that come with a guarantee of success. First, the recipes always work – just follow the instructions and you too will get the results you see in the photographs. Second, and perhaps more importantly, they are delicious – created by experienced home economists and chefs, all triple-tested and, thanks to their straightforward instructions, easy to make.

British and North American readers:
Please note that Australian cup and spoon
measurements are metric. A quick
conversion guide appears on page 119.

When I was a girl, a salad consisted of iceberg lettuce shredded beyond
recognition, mealy sliced tomatoes and canned beetroot, all doused in a
vinegar so acidic the memory still puckers my mouth. Well, as they say,
we've come a long way, baby, in a comparatively short period of time.

Today, mesclun and rocket, balsamic vinegar and extra virgin olive oil are
found on restaurant menus everywhere as well as in the vast majority of our
kitchens, and the ingredients we choose to assemble into salads can come
from any and every food category: cereals, breads and grains; meat, poultry
and seafood; fruits, seeds and nuts — the beauty of the salad that we now
know is that there are no barriers regarding its content or its presentation.

I hope you'll be inspired by the delicious recipes you'll discover within
these pages — *Salads: simple, fast and fresh* is a book that is as innovative
as the subject itself.

Pamela Clark

FOOD EDITOR

contents

leafy greens

ROCKET

RADICCHIO

GREEN CORAL LETTUCE

MESCLUN

RED MIGNONET

RED CORAL LETTUCE

CURLY ENDIVE

BABY SPINACH

SILVERBEET
(OR SWISS CHARD)

ICEBERG LETTUCE

leafy greens

BUTTER
LETTUCE

RED OAK LEAF LETTUCE

MIZUNA

COS LETTUCE

GREEN
OAK LEAF
LETTUCE

WHITE AND RED WITLOF (OR BELGIAN ENDIVE)

BABY
COS LETTUCE

LAMB'S LETTUCE
(OR MÂCHE OR
CORN SALAD)

sprouts
and cresses

MUSTARD SPROUTS
(OR MUSTARD CRESS)

WATERCRESS

MUNG BEAN SPROUTS

SNOW PEA TENDRILS

ALFALFA SPROUTS

SNOW PEA SPROUTS

asian greens

BOK CHOY
(OR PAK CHOI
OR CHINESE CHARD)

BABY BOK CHOY

WATER SPINACH
(OR KANGKUNG)

CHOY SUM
(OR FLOWERING
CABBAGE)

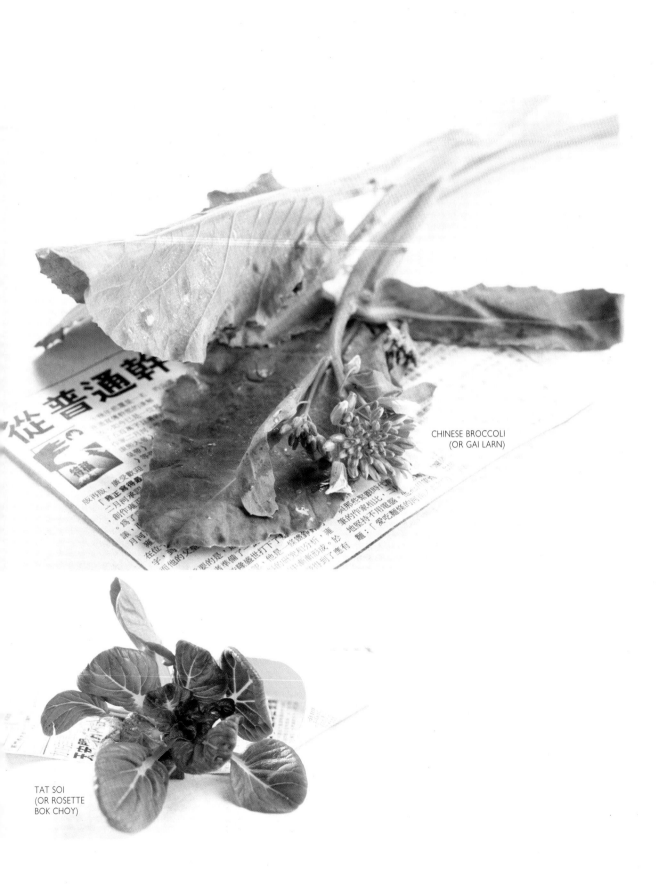

CHINESE BROCCOLI
(OR GAI LARN)

TAT SOI
(OR ROSETTE
BOK CHOY)

tomatoes, mushrooms and cucumbers

TEARDROP TOMATOES

EGG TOMATOES

CHERRY TOMATOES

VINE-RIPENED TOMATOES

GREEN TOMATOES

SHIITAKE MUSHROOMS

SWISS BROWN (OR ROMAN OR CREMINI) MUSHROOMS

BUTTON MUSHROOMS

FLAT (OR FIELD) MUSHROOMS

TELEGRAPH CUCUMBERS

GREEN CUCUMBER

LEBANESE CUCUMBERS

dressings

If you prefer, you can blend or process these dressings — or use a hand blender — rather than shake them in a jar. This gives the dressings a slightly thicker, creamier consistency.

Adding oil to dressing

The basic dressing ingredients

Shaking the dressing well

french dressing

1/4 cup (60ml) white vinegar
3/4 cup (180ml) olive oil
1/2 teaspoon sugar
1 teaspoon Dijon mustard

Combine ingredients in screw-top jar; shake well.

MAKES ABOUT 1 CUP (250ML)

per tablespoon 14.3g fat; 535kJ

guilt-free dressing

1/2 cup buttermilk
2 tablespoons finely chopped fresh chives
2 tablespoons no-oil French dressing
1 tablespoon seeded mustard
1 tablespoon honey

Combine ingredients in screw-top jar; shake well.

MAKES ABOUT 2/3 CUP (160ML)

per tablespoon 0.4g fat; 944kJ

fresh tomato sauce

3 large (270g) egg tomatoes, peeled, seeded, quartered
2 green onions, chopped coarsely
1/3 cup (80ml) red wine vinegar
1/3 cup (80ml) sweet chilli sauce
2 cloves garlic, quartered
1 teaspoon seeded mustard
1 teaspoon sugar
1 teaspoon cracked black pepper
1/4 cup coarsely chopped fresh parsley

Blend or process ingredients until almost smooth.

MAKES ABOUT 1 1/4 CUPS (310ML)

per tablespoon 0.2g fat; 45kJ

italian dressing

2 tablespoons white wine vinegar
2 tablespoons lemon juice
1/2 teaspoon sugar
2 cloves garlic, crushed
3/4 cup (180ml) olive oil
1 tablespoon finely chopped fresh basil leaves
1 tablespoon finely chopped fresh oregano leaves

Combine ingredients in screw-top jar; shake well.

MAKES ABOUT 1 CUP (250ML)

per tablespoon 14.3g fat; 538kJ

opposite: french dressing (*above left*)
fresh tomato sauce (*above right*)
guilt-free dressing (*below left*)
italian dressing (*below right*)

... and mayonnaise

Mayonnaise is traditionally made using a bowl and whisk, adding the oil drop by drop at first, then in a thin stream. However, if you're in a hurry, using a blender or food processor is faster. Note that this makes a much thicker sauce, which we suggest thinning with a little milk or water. We used a combination of light and regular olive oil; you can vary the proportions to suit your taste, or the food it will accompany.

Whisking egg yolks

Adding combined oils

Thinning mayonnaise with milk

basic mayonnaise

2 egg yolks
1 tablespoon lemon juice
1/2 teaspoon salt
1/2 teaspoon dry mustard
1/2 cup (125ml) light olive oil
1/4 cup (125ml) olive oil

Whisk, blend or process egg yolks, juice, salt and mustard until smooth. Add combined oils gradually in thin stream while motor is operating; blend until thick.

MAKES ABOUT 3/4 CUP (180ML)

per tablespoon 27.7g fat; 1040kJ

thousand island mayonnaise

1/3 cup (80ml) tomato paste
1/3 cup (80ml) tomato sauce
1 tablespoon Worcestershire sauce
1/2 teaspoon Tabasco sauce
3/4 cup (180ml) basic mayonnaise

Whisk paste and sauces into basic mayonnaise.

MAKES ABOUT 11/4 CUPS (310ML)

per tablespoon 16.7g fat; 668kJ

curried mayonnaise

1 tablespoon curry powder
3/4 cup (180ml) basic mayonnaise

Add powder to dry pan, stir over heat until fragrant; cool. Whisk into basic mayonnaise.

MAKES ABOUT 3/4 CUP (180ML)

per tablespoon 27.9g fat; 1054kJ

herb mayonnaise

2 tablespoons chopped fresh chives
2 tablespoons chopped fresh parsley
2 tablespoons chopped fresh basil leaves
3/4 cup (180ml) basic mayonnaise

Whisk herbs into basic mayonnaise.

MAKES ABOUT 3/4 CUP (180ML)

per tablespoon 27.7g fat; 1041kJ

garlic mayonnaise

3 cloves garlic, quartered
1 quantity basic mayonnaise ingredients

Blend or process garlic with egg yolks, juice, salt and mustard until smooth. Proceed with method for basic mayonnaise.

MAKES ABOUT 3/4 CUP (180ML)

per tablespoon 27.7g fat; 1044kJ

opposite: thousand island mayonnaise (*above left*);
curried mayonnaise (*above right*); herb mayonnaise
(*below left*); garlic mayonnaise (*below right*)

classics

These traditional recipes hail from all around the world and are so undeniably good that, through the generations, their appeal has never diminished — they are, in a word, classics.

caesar salad

PREPARATION TIME 25 MINUTES • COOKING TIME 5 MINUTES

This universally loved salad is thought to have originated in Tijuana, Mexico, in the 1920s, in a restaurant owned by an Italian chef by the name of Caesar Cardini.

7 slices thick white bread
2 tablespoons light olive oil
100g parmesan cheese
1 large cos lettuce
5 whole canned anchovy fillets,
   drained, halved lengthways

CAESAR DRESSING

1 egg
1 clove garlic, crushed
2 tablespoons lemon juice
1/2 teaspoon Dijon mustard
5 whole canned anchovy fillets, drained
3/4 cup (180ml) light olive oil

Browning croutons

1 Discard crusts; cut bread into 1cm cubes. Heat the oil in large pan; cook bread, stirring, until browned and crisp. Drain croutons on absorbent paper.

2 Using vegetable peeler, shave cheese into long thin pieces.

Shaving parmesan flakes

3 Combine torn lettuce leaves with half of the croutons, half the anchovies and half the cheese in large bowl; add half of the dressing, mix well. Sprinkle remaining croutons, anchovies and cheese over salad; drizzle with remaining dressing.

caesar dressing Blend or process egg, garlic, juice, mustard and anchovies until smooth; with motor operating, add oil in thin stream, process until dressing thickens.

SERVES 4

per serve 65.1g fat; 3335kJ

serving suggestion Caesar salad can be served as a light meal on its own or, as you see in many restaurants, with pieces of grilled chicken breast tossed in with the dressing.

tip The caesar dressing can be made a day ahead. Cover and refrigerate until needed.

Adding oil to thicken dressing

BABY (TOP) AND REGULAR-SIZE COS LETTUCES

Stringing the celery

Removing walnut meat from shells

waldorf salad

PREPARATION TIME 15 MINUTES

A "signature" dish from the United States, Waldorf salad was created at the beginning of the 20th century by chefs at New York's world-famous Waldorf-Astoria hotel, and proved so popular that it rapidly became a staple in kitchens throughout America.

**4 medium (600g) red
   delicious apples**
¼ cup (60ml) lemon juice
5 trimmed (375g) celery sticks
**1 cup (120g) coarsely
   chopped walnuts**

MAYONNAISE

2 egg yolks
2 teaspoons lemon juice
1 teaspoon Dijon mustard
¾ cup (180ml) olive oil
1 tablespoon warm water

1 Core and coarsely chop unpeeled apples. Combine apple in small bowl with juice.

2 Coarsely chop celery.

3 Combine apple, celery and walnuts in large serving bowl with mayonnaise. Serve salad in lettuce leaves, if desired.

mayonnaise Blend or process egg yolks, juice and mustard until smooth; with motor operating, add oil in thin stream, process until mayonnaise thickens. Stir in the water.

SERVES 4

per serve 63g fat; 2776kJ

serving suggestion Serve Waldorf salad with roast chicken to continue the American theme.

tips Use warm water if the mayonnaise needs to be thinned, because it will blend into the mixture more easily.

• Mayonnaise can be made a day ahead and kept, covered, under refrigeration until needed.

RED DELICIOUS APPLE

chicken larb

PREPARATION TIME 20 MINUTES • COOKING TIME 15 MINUTES

This delicious Thai salad originates from the north-western province around Chiang Mai; it can be made with beef or pork mince as well as the chicken version given below.

2 tablespoons peanut oil

1 tablespoon finely chopped fresh lemon grass

2 red Thai chillies, seeded, chopped finely

1 clove garlic, crushed

1 tablespoon grated fresh ginger

750g minced chicken

4 kaffir lime leaves

1 tablespoon fish sauce

1/3 cup (80ml) lime juice

1 medium (150g) white onion, sliced thinly

1 cup loosely packed fresh coriander leaves

100g bean sprouts, tips trimmed

1/2 cup loosely packed fresh Thai basil leaves

1/2 cup loosely packed fresh Vietnamese mint leaves

100g watercress

1 medium (170g) green cucumber, sliced thinly

1 tablespoon finely chopped fresh Vietnamese mint leaves, extra

1 Heat half of the oil in large pan; cook lemon grass, chilli, garlic and ginger, stirring, until fragrant. Add chicken; cook, stirring, about 10 minutes or until cooked through.

2 Add torn lime leaves, half of the fish sauce and half of the lime juice; cook, stirring, 5 minutes.

3 Combine onion, coriander, sprouts, basil, mint, watercress and cucumber in large bowl; drizzle with combined remaining fish sauce, juice and oil, toss salad mixture gently.

4 Place salad mixture on serving plate, top with chicken mixture; sprinkle with extra mint.

SERVES 4

per serve 17.7g fat; 1446kJ

serving suggestion Hot and sour soup is a good opening act for a big platter of larb.

tip Add the minced chicken to pan in batches, stirring between additions, so chicken doesn't clump.

Finely chopping lemon grass

Seeding and chopping red Thai chillies

THAI BASIL

mermaid's tresses

PREPARATION TIME 30 MINUTES • COOKING TIME 10 MINUTES

We used shredded Chinese broccoli in this recipe, but you can substitute spinach or any Asian or spring greens. The secret is to ensure your finely shredded greens are completely dry before deep-frying or they will cause the oil to splatter.

1kg Chinese broccoli

2 teaspoons brown sugar

2 teaspoons water

1/2 cup (75g) roasted unsalted cashews

2 teaspoons white sesame seeds

1 Chinese dried scallop

vegetable oil, for deep-frying

1 teaspoon sugar

1/2 teaspoon salt

1 Trim stems and hard veins from broccoli; shred broccoli leaves finely.

2 Combine brown sugar and the water in medium pan; cook, stirring, until sugar dissolves. Add nuts and seeds; cook, stirring, until coated in sugar mixture. Place on oiled oven tray; cool.

3 Shred scallop finely.

4 Heat the oil in large pan; deep-fry broccoli, in batches, until crisp. Drain on absorbent paper; sprinkle with combined sugar and salt. Place mermaid's tresses in serving bowl; sprinkle with nuts and scallop.

SERVES 6

per serve 7.4g fat; 476kJ (excludes oil for deep-frying)

serving suggestion Serve immediately (so tresses remain crisp) as a first course for a main of Cantonese steamed snapper, chilli chicken wings or Mongolian lamb.

tip Chinese dried scallops are sold in Asian food stores as conpoy; if required, they can be reconstituted in cold water and used as an ingredient in various stir-fries.

Finely shredding broccoli

Cashews coated in seeds and sugar

Sprinkling sugar and salt over tresses

DRIED SCALLOPS (CONPOY)

vietnamese chicken and cabbage salad

PREPARATION TIME 20 MINUTES • COOKING TIME 5 MINUTES

This dish, called Ga Xe Phai, is one of the most popular salads in Vietnam. You will need a 1kg barbecued chicken and 2 medium (240g) carrots for this recipe.

COOKED (TOP) AND UNCOOKED PRAWN CRACKERS

1 Heat oil in medium pan; deep-fry crackers, in batches, until puffed. Drain on absorbent paper.

2 Combine chicken, cabbage, onion, carrot and mint in large bowl; drizzle with chilli lime dressing, mix well.

3 Sprinkle coriander leaves over salad; serve with prawn crackers.

chilli lime dressing Combine all ingredients in screw-top jar; shake well.

SERVES 4

per serve 14.3g fat; 1053kJ (excludes oil for deep-frying)

serving suggestion Serve this salad as part of a Vietnamese banquet – it goes well with Chicken and Cellophane-Noodle Soup.

tips The prawn crackers can be cooked 2 days ahead; store in an airtight container.

• To lower the fat count, cook the prawn crackers in microwave oven. Place 10 prawn crackers around the edge of turntable; cook, uncovered, on HIGH (100%) about 30 seconds or until puffed.

vegetable oil, for deep-frying

12 (20g) prawn crackers

2¹/₂ cups (375g) shredded cooked chicken

4 cups (320g) shredded white cabbage

1 medium (150g) brown onion, sliced thinly

1 cup coarsely grated carrot

¹/₂ cup coarsely chopped fresh Vietnamese mint

2 tablespoons fresh coriander leaves

CHILLI LIME DRESSING

2 cloves garlic, crushed

1 red Thai chilli, chopped finely

1 tablespoon rice vinegar

2 tablespoons lime juice

2 tablespoons peanut oil

1 tablespoon fish sauce

2 teaspoons sugar

gado gado

PREPARATION TIME 1 HOUR • COOKING TIME 35 MINUTES

Gado gado translates roughly as "mixed mixed" which helps explain the casual way Indonesians eat this salad. Each diner makes his or her personal selection from the assortment of vegetables then mixes them together, dollops on the peanut sauce and mixes the salad again. Gado gado can be eaten at room temperature or cold. Substitute fresh ginger for the galangal if the latter is not available.

2 medium (400g) potatoes,
    sliced thickly

2 medium (240g) carrots,
    sliced thickly

150g green beans, chopped

1/2 small (600g) green cabbage

vegetable oil, for deep-frying

300g firm tofu, cut
    into 2cm cubes

2 medium (380g) tomatoes,
    cut into wedges

2 (260g) Lebanese cucumbers,
    sliced thickly

2 cups (160g) bean sprouts

4 hard-boiled eggs, quartered

PEANUT SAUCE

1 cup (150g) roasted
    unsalted peanuts

1 tablespoon peanut oil

1 small (80g) brown onion,
    chopped finely

1 clove garlic, crushed

3 red Thai chillies, seeded,
    chopped finely

1 tablespoon finely
    grated fresh galangal

1 tablespoon lime juice

1 tablespoon brown sugar

1/2 teaspoon shrimp paste

1 cup (250ml) coconut milk

1/4 teaspoon thick
    tamarind concentrate

1 tablespoon ketjap manis

1 Boil, steam or microwave potato, carrot and beans, separately, until potato is cooked through and carrot and beans are just tender.

2 Meanwhile, drop cabbage leaves into large pan of boiling water; remove leaves and quickly plunge into cold water. Drain cabbage; slice finely.

3 Heat oil in small pan; deep-fry tofu, in batches, until browned. Drain on absorbent paper.

4 Place potato, carrot, beans, cabbage, tofu, tomato, cucumber, sprouts and egg in sections on serving plate; serve with peanut sauce.

peanut sauce Process nuts until chopped coarsely. Heat the oil in small pan; cook onion, garlic and chilli, stirring, until onion is golden brown. Add peanuts and remaining ingredients; bring to boil. Simmer 5 minutes or until mixture thickens; cool 10 minutes. Pour sauce into small bowl and serve with vegetable salad.

SERVES 4

per serve 47g fat; 2990kJ (excludes oil for deep-frying)

serving suggestion Serve as a vegetarian snack or with rice and chicken, fish, shellfish, lamb or beef.

Deep-frying tofu

Chopping green beans and cucumber

Grating fresh galangal

Peeling beetroot

Cutting potato and beetroot into wedges

russian beetroot salad

PREPARATION TIME 20 MINUTES • COOKING TIME 40 MINUTES

We used fresh beetroot and peas in this recipe, but you can use canned whole baby beetroot and frozen peas, if desired. You will need approximately 450g fresh peas-in-the-pod to give 180g of shelled peas. To lower the fat count, use the reduced-fat, instead of the full-fat, version of sour cream.

4 medium (700g) fresh beetroot

3 medium (600g) potatoes

1 cup (180g) shelled fresh peas

1 small (100g) red onion, chopped finely

SOUR CREAM DRESSING

1 egg yolk

2 teaspoons Dijon mustard

2 teaspoons white vinegar

1/2 cup (125ml) olive oil

1/2 cup (125ml) sour cream

1 Wrap trimmed beetroot, separately, in foil; bake in hot oven 40 minutes or until tender. Cool 10 minutes; peel, cut into wedges.

2 Meanwhile, peel potatoes; cut into wedges. Boil, steam or microwave potato and peas, separately, until just tender; drain.

3 Place beetroot, potato, peas, onion and sour cream dressing in large bowl; toss gently to combine. Serve warm or chilled.

sour cream dressing Blend or process egg yolk, mustard and vinegar until smooth. With motor operating, add oil in thin stream; process until dressing thickens. Transfer dressing to small bowl, stir in sour cream.

SERVES 4

per serve 43.9g fat; 2324kJ

serving suggestion Goes well with beef or lamb dishes.

tips We used sebago (brushed) potatoes in this recipe because they don't disintegrate when cooked. Potatoes and beetroot can be cooked a day ahead; cover, refrigerate until ready to assemble salad.

• Trim beetroot, leaving about 1cm at both stem and root ends; avoid piercing the beetroot as colour will leach.

SEBAGO (BRUSHED) POTATOES

27

salade niçoise

PREPARATION TIME 1 HOUR • COOKING TIME 5 MINUTES

There are many versions of this popular dish, but an authentic Salade niçoise (originally from the Provençal city of Nice) always includes ingredients that speak of this sun-kissed region of France: tomatoes, capers, olives and garlic. A typical recipe also includes tuna, anchovies, egg and raw vegetables.

1 medium (170g) red onion

4 medium (300g) egg tomatoes

3 trimmed (225g) celery sticks

3 hard-boiled eggs

200g green beans

12 whole canned anchovy fillets, drained, halved lengthways

425g can tuna in oil, drained, flaked

100g niçoise olives

2 tablespoons baby capers

2 tablespoons shredded basil leaves

LEMON GARLIC DRESSING

1/2 cup (125ml) extra virgin olive oil

1/4 cup (60ml) lemon juice

1 clove garlic, crushed

1 teaspoon sugar

1 Quarter onion lengthways; slice thinly. Cut tomatoes into wedges; remove seeds. Slice celery thinly. Shell and quarter eggs.

2 Top and tail beans; boil, steam or microwave beans until just tender, drain. Rinse beans under cold water; drain well.

3 Layer onion, tomato, celery, egg, beans, anchovy and tuna on serving plate. Sprinkle with olives, capers and basil; drizzle with lemon garlic dressing.

lemon garlic dressing Combine all ingredients in screw-top jar; shake well.

SERVES 4

per serve 50.3g fat; 2646kJ

serving suggestion In France, this salad is often served on its own as a light meal, accompanied by warm crusty bread and a glass of light red wine. As a first course, it goes well with barbecued fish or other grilled seafood.

tip Niçoise olives, tiny ovate brown-black olives with a rich nutty flavour, are grown all over the rough, hilly terrain of Provence. You'll find them in some supermarkets and delicatessens. If unavailable, substitute any small brown olive.

NIÇOISE OLIVES

Shredding basil

Layering vegetables on plate

tunisian tuna salad

PREPARATION TIME 30 MINUTES

This colourful salad from the Tunisian capital of Tunis tastes as good as it looks. Unlike the people on the other side of the Mediterranean, North Africans like their food highly spiced and, while this recipe only includes two chillies, you can increase or decrease the quantity as you like.

Seeding a tomato

2 hard-boiled eggs

1 medium (200g) green capsicum, chopped finely

2 medium (380g) tomatoes, seeded, chopped finely

4 green onions, chopped finely

2 large canned anchovy fillets, drained, chopped finely

10 (30g) seeded green olives, chopped finely

2 red Thai chillies, seeded, chopped finely

2 teaspoons finely chopped fresh mint leaves

185g can tuna, drained, flaked

1 tablespoon baby capers, drained

HARISSA-STYLE DRESSING

2 tablespoons olive oil

1 clove garlic, crushed

1 teaspoon coriander seeds

1 teaspoon caraway seeds

1 tablespoon lemon juice

2 tablespoons red wine vinegar

Cutting olives, ready to seed

1 Shell hard-boiled eggs; chop finely.

2 Combine eggs with remaining ingredients in medium bowl; drizzle dressing over salad, toss gently to combine.

harissa-style dressing Heat the oil in small pan, add garlic and seeds; cook, stirring, until fragrant. Stir in juice and vinegar.

SERVES 4

per serve 14.3g fat; 886kJ

serving suggestion Great eaten on its own with a fresh and crunchy French stick or, for a quick snack, roll up some of this salad in flat bread, like pitta or lavash, and eat with your hands.

tip You can omit the canned tuna and serve the salad with fresh char-grilled tuna.

Cooking garlic and seeds in hot oil

BABY CAPERS

Slicing chicken diagonally

Whisking mayonnaise mixture

coronation chicken

PREPARATION TIME 20 MINUTES • COOKING TIME 30 MINUTES

*Created for the coronation of Queen Elizabeth II in 1953, this creamy salad
is made tangy with mango chutney and curry powder. Shredded barbecued chicken
can be substituted for the cooked sliced chicken breasts, if desired.*

1 tablespoon olive oil

850g chicken breast fillets

1/2 cup (125ml) mayonnaise

1/2 cup (125ml) sour cream

1/4 cup (90g) mango chutney

2 teaspoons curry powder

300g white seedless grapes

**1 cup (100g) walnuts,
    chopped coarsely**

125g snow pea sprouts

1 Heat oil in large pan; cook chicken, in batches, until browned both sides.

2 Place chicken in shallow medium baking dish; cover, bake in moderate oven about 20 minutes or until cooked through. Cool 10 minutes; cut diagonally into 5mm-wide slices.

3 Place mayonnaise, sour cream, chutney and curry powder in small bowl; whisk until smooth.

4 Remove grapes from stems.

5 Gently toss chicken with grapes, nuts and mayonnaise mixture in large bowl; serve with snow pea sprouts.

SERVES 6

per serve 33g fat; 2128kJ

serving suggestion Serve rolled in fresh lavash or pitta bread for a tasty lunch idea, with a crisp garden salad.

tips The mayonnaise mixture can be made a day ahead; keep, covered, in refrigerator. Chicken is best prepared on the day of serving. We used Thompson seedless grapes as these large grapes are particularly juicy.

• This salad will taste even better with your own homemade mayonnaise. Blend or process 2 egg yolks, 2 teaspoons lemon juice and 1 teaspoon Dijon mustard until smooth. With motor operating, add 3/4 cup (180ml) light olive oil in thin stream; process until mayonnaise thickens. Thin with 1 tablespoon warm water, if necessary.

THOMPSON SEEDLESS GRAPES

---

spinach, bacon and crouton salad

PREPARATION TIME 25 MINUTES • COOKING TIME 20 MINUTES

This American salad is popular with ladies who lunch! We used extra thin bacon rashers; you can substitute prosciutto if you wish.

1 small French stick
1 clove garlic, crushed
1/4 cup (60ml) olive oil
10 (320g) extra thin
  bacon rashers
1 egg yolk
2 teaspoons Dijon mustard
1/4 teaspoon Tabasco sauce
1 tablespoon white wine vinegar
2 teaspoons lemon juice
2 tablespoons cream
1 clove garlic, crushed, extra
1/2 cup (125ml) extra
  virgin olive oil
400g baby spinach leaves
5 hard-boiled eggs

1 Cut bread in half lengthways, cut halves into 5mm slices; place in single layer on oven tray. Brush bread slices on one side with combined garlic and olive oil; toast in moderate oven about 8 minutes or until croutons are browned lightly.

2 Remove rind and trim fat from bacon; cut rashers into quarters. Cook in heated oiled large pan until crisp; drain on absorbent paper. When bacon is cold, crumble.

3 Combine yolk, mustard, sauce, vinegar, juice, cream and extra garlic in small bowl. Gradually whisk in the extra virgin olive oil. Gently toss spinach and dressing in large serving bowl.

4 Shell hard-boiled eggs; chop coarsely. Add eggs, croutons and bacon to serving bowl; toss gently to combine.

SERVES 6

per serve 30.3g fat; 1613kJ

serving suggestion Pack up the family, this salad and some sausages to barbecue and head to the park. All ingredients can be prepared ahead of time then packed, separately; combine when you're ready to eat.

tip To keep spinach crisp, pick the freshest leaves and rinse under cold water. Shake, then place in an airtight plastic bag and refrigerate for several hours or overnight.

Slicing French bread

Separating egg

baby beetroot with skordalia

PREPARATION TIME 15 MINUTES • COOKING TIME 40 MINUTES

It's said that more vegetables per capita are consumed in Greece than any other western country. We don't know if this is fact or fiction, but Greeks certainly enjoy cooking a variety of vegetables in many different ways. This traditional Greek beetroot salad is a popular dish, which is usually served with skordalia, a delicious garlic sauce.

1.8kg fresh baby beetroot

1 clove garlic, crushed

1/4 cup (60ml) olive oil

2 tablespoons red wine vinegar

SKORDALIA

2 medium (400g) potatoes

4 slices stale white bread

6 cloves garlic, crushed

1/4 cup (60ml) olive oil

2 tablespoons lemon juice

1 Discard beetroot stems and leaves. Boil, steam or microwave unpeeled beetroot until just tender; drain. Cool 10 minutes; peel while warm, cut each beetroot in half.

2 Place beetroot on serving plate; pour over combined remaining ingredients. Serve with skordalia.

skordalia Boil, steam or microwave potatoes until just tender; drain, mash well. Discard crusts from bread, soak bread in cold water 2 minutes; drain, squeeze water from bread. Blend or process bread, potato and garlic until smooth. With motor operating, add the combined oil and juice in thin stream; process until sauce thickens.

BABY BEETROOT

SERVES 4

per serve 30g fat; 2362kJ

serving suggestion Lamb is the most popular meat in Greece and goes particularly well with this salad. Try it with a roast leg of lamb or souvlakia (garlic and lemon lamb kebabs).

Boiling unpeeled beetroot

Squeezing water from bread

Pouring in combined oil and juice

Dry-frying bacon

Chopping gherkins

german hot potato salad

PREPARATION TIME 10 MINUTES • COOKING TIME 15 MINUTES

Typical hearty German fare, this classic salad has been made easier to prepare by the addition of ready-made mayonnaise; however, if you prefer, you can make your own.

4 eggs

4 bacon rashers, chopped

750g tiny new potatoes

2 pickled gherkins, chopped finely

1 tablespoon finely chopped fresh flat-leaf parsley

2/3 cup (160ml) mayonnaise

1/3 cup (80ml) sour cream

2 teaspoons lemon juice

1 Cover eggs with water in medium pan; bring to boil. Simmer, uncovered, 10 minutes; drain. Cool eggs under cold water; shell and halve.

2 Meanwhile, fry bacon, uncovered, in dry heated pan until browned and crisp; drain on absorbent paper.

3 Boil, steam or microwave potatoes until tender; drain and halve.

4 Combine remaining ingredients in large pan; stir over low heat until just hot. Place mayonnaise mixture in large bowl with potato, bacon and egg; toss gently to combine.

SERVES 4

per serve 31g fat; 2106kJ

serving suggestion This warm, satisfying salad is great served with grilled pork chops and hot and sour red cabbage.

tip Bacon can be fried and eggs hard-boiled a few hours beforehand as long as the potato halves and mayonnaise dressing are hot just before serving time.

TINY NEW POTATOES

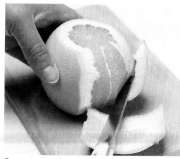

Removing peel and pith from orange

Alternating slices of orange and radish

moroccan orange and radish salad

PREPARATION TIME 30 MINUTES

This piquant salad is the ideal contrast to the rich flavours of Moroccan tagines – the meat, poultry or fish stews that are a fundamental part of Moroccan cooking. We used large round red radishes for this recipe, however you can substitute the longer, white variety, known as daikon.

6 large (1.8kg) seedless oranges

4 large (200g) red radishes

1/2 small (50g) red onion, sliced finely

1 cup (180g) Niçoise olives, seeded

LEMON DRESSING

1 clove garlic, crushed

1/2 teaspoon sweet paprika

1/2 teaspoon ground cumin

2 tablespoons lemon juice

2 tablespoons olive oil

1/4 teaspoon sugar

2 tablespoons finely chopped fresh parsley

1 teaspoon orange-flower water

1/2 teaspoon ground cinnamon

1 Peel oranges, removing white pith; slice thinly. Slice radishes thinly.

2 Overlap alternate slices of orange and radish around edge of serving plate; overlap remaining slices in centre. Top with onion and olives; drizzle with dressing.

lemon dressing Combine all ingredients in screw-top jar; shake well.

SERVES 4

per serve 11.4g fat; 1020kJ

serving suggestion This refreshing salad is often eaten as part of a first course spread in Morocco, but it's also an ideal accompaniment to a rich tagine of meat, poultry or fish. It's also great with grilled meats or kebabs.

tip Orange-flower water is often used in Moroccan cooking for its cooling effect. In this salad, a teaspoon of fragrant orange-flower water is used to sweeten the sharp taste of the radish. You can buy bottles of orange-flower water at selected supermarkets and delicatessens.

ORANGE-FLOWER WATER

fattoush

PREPARATION TIME 15 MINUTES • COOKING TIME 15 MINUTES

Most cultures have a salad that incorporates yesterday's bread as an ingredient (rather than wasting it), and fattoush is a delectable Middle-Eastern version. Purslane, a leafy green that grows wild, is often commonly called pigweed and can be hard to find in shops; substitute it with baby rocket leaves in this recipe.

2 large pieces pitta

1 tablespoon olive oil

2 (260g) Lebanese cucumbers,
   sliced thinly

4 medium (760g) tomatoes,
   sliced thinly

3 green onions, sliced thinly

1 medium (200g) green capsicum,
   chopped finely

1 cup coarsely chopped fresh
   flat-leaf parsley

1/4 cup coarsely chopped
   fresh mint leaves

1 cup coarsely chopped
   fresh purslane

2 tablespoons olive oil, extra

1/4 cup (60ml) lemon juice

1 clove garlic, crushed

1 Brush bread both sides with the oil, place on oven tray; toast in moderately hot oven about 15 minutes or until crisp. Cool; break bread into small pieces.

2 Combine cucumber, tomato, onion, capsicum and herbs in large bowl. Just before serving, add bread; drizzle fattoush with combined extra oil, juice and garlic.

SERVES 4

per serve 16.3g fat; 1173kJ

serving suggestion Fattoush is usually served, rather than the more common tabbouleh, as part of a mezze; it's also good served with "ful medames" – dried broad beans stewed with lashings of garlic and lemon juice until almost a puree.

tip The toasted pitta pieces can be made a day ahead. Store in airtight container until needed.

PURSLANE

Breaking toasted pitta

Chopping flat-leaf parsley and mint

tabbouleh

PREPARATION TIME 40 MINUTES (plus refrigeration time)

Tabbouleh is one Middle-Eastern salad we're all familiar with these days – besides being absolutely delicious, it's one of the most nutritionally sound dishes we can think of, containing plenty of fibre as well as healthy proportions of Vitamin C.

3 medium (570g) tomatoes

1/2 cup (80g) burghul

**5 cups tightly packed fresh
    flat-leaf parsley**

1 medium (170g) red onion

**1 cup tightly packed
    fresh mint leaves**

1/4 cup (60ml) lemon juice

**1/4 cup (60ml) extra
    virgin olive oil**

1 Chop tomatoes finely, retaining as much of the juice as possible. Place tomato and juice on top of burghul in small bowl, cover; refrigerate at least 2 hours or until burghul is soft.

2 Meanwhile, cut parsley coarsely with scissors or chop coarsely with knife; chop onion finely, chop mint coarsely. Keep chopped ingredients separate.

3 Combine parsley, onion and mint in large bowl with burghul-tomato mixture and remaining ingredients; toss gently to combine.

SERVES 4

per serve 14.9g fat; 862kJ

serving suggestions Tabbouleh is the ideal accompaniment to any Middle-Eastern meal. Serve it with garlic chicken, beef or lamb skewers, or baked fish. You can also serve it as part of a mezze (hors d'oeuvres); place a little tabbouleh in a lettuce leaf, roll up like a cigar and eat it with your fingers.

tip Burghul, often mistakenly thought to be the same as cracked wheat, is a wheat kernel that has been steamed, dried and crushed. It comes in a variety of grinds – coarse, medium and fine – and can be bought from health food stores, delicatessens and supermarkets under various names: bulgar, bulghur wheat or Lebanese crushed wheat. Do not substitute with ordinary unprocessed cracked wheat.

FLAT-LEAF PARSLEY

Placing tomato onto burghul

Cutting parsley leaves with scissors

thai beef salad

PREPARATION TIME 25 MINUTES • COOKING TIME 7 MINUTES (plus resting time)

400g beef rump steak

2 small (160g) white onions, sliced thinly

2 (260g) Lebanese cucumbers, seeded, sliced thinly

1 red Thai chilli, seeded, sliced thinly

250g cherry tomatoes, halved

1/4 cup loosely packed fresh basil leaves

1/4 cup loosely packed fresh coriander leaves

1/4 cup loosely packed fresh Vietnamese mint leaves

GARLIC DRESSING

2 red Thai chillies, seeded, chopped coarsely

2 tablespoons coarsely chopped fresh lemon grass

2/3 cup firmly packed fresh coriander leaves

3 cloves garlic, chopped coarsely

1/3 cup (80ml) lime juice

1 tablespoon fish sauce

1 tablespoon soy sauce

1 Cook beef in heated oiled grill pan (or on grill or barbecue) until browned both sides and cooked as desired (in Thailand, to medium rare); cover, rest 10 minutes, slice thinly.

2 Just before serving, gently toss beef, remaining ingredients and dressing in large bowl.

garlic dressing Blend or process all ingredients until smooth.

SERVES 4

per serve 7g fat; 800kJ

serving suggestion This is a great first course when you feel like preparing a special Thai banquet for your friends.

tip Vietnamese mint (also sometimes sold as laksa leaves or Cambodian mint) has long pointy leaves and is quite dark green in colour. It is most frequently used uncooked in salads or stirred into soups (like laksa or pho), and is often eaten, like lettuce leaves, as an antidote to exceptionally chilli-hot foods.

• Increase the heat of this dish if you want to by adding more than one chilli. Thai chillies are sometimes referred to as "scuds", as they seem to carry almost as much firepower as a missile; you can substitute a milder chilli if you wish.

Slicing beef thinly

Removing herb leaves from stems

VIETNAMESE MINT

Deveining a prawn

Separating yolk from egg white

prawn cocktail

PREPARATION TIME 45 MINUTES

We've given the '70s icon a makeover for the new millennium. Fresh, flavoursome prawns and a crisp and crunchy wedge of perfect iceberg lettuce are presented side by side – no soggy leaves or confusion of flavours here.

36 medium (900g) cooked prawns
1 medium iceberg lettuce

COCKTAIL DRESSING

2 egg yolks
1 tablespoon white vinegar
1 tablespoon Dijon mustard
1 cup (250ml) olive oil
1 teaspoon Tabasco sauce
1 tablespoon Worcestershire sauce
1/4 cup (60ml) tomato sauce
2 teaspoons lemon juice

1 Shell and devein prawns, leaving heads and tails intact.

2 Cut lettuce into 6 wedges.

3 Just before serving, divide prawns and lettuce among serving plates; drizzle with dressing.

cocktail dressing Blend or process egg yolks, vinegar and mustard until smooth; with motor operating, add oil in thin stream, process until dressing thickens. Stir in sauces and juice.

SERVES 6

per serve 42g fat; 2000kJ

serving suggestion Perfect as a first course for a lazy Sunday lunch – followed by a steak off the barbie – or for an elegant supper preceding a standing rib roast.

tip You can also serve the dressing on its own, as a dipping sauce for prawns or pan-fried fish fillets.

ICEBERG LETTUCE LEAF

panzanella

PREPARATION TIME 25 MINUTES

Panzanella is a traditional Italian bread salad that probably came about as a way of using up yesterday's bread. For this recipe, we used ciabatta, a wood-fired white loaf readily available from most supermarkets, but any Italian crusty bread may be used in its place.

1 long loaf stale ciabatta
6 medium (1.1kg) tomatoes
2 trimmed (150g) celery sticks
1 (130g) Lebanese cucumber
1 medium (170g) red onion
1/4 cup (60ml) red wine vinegar
1/2 cup (125ml) olive oil
1 clove garlic, crushed
1/4 cup finely shredded fresh basil leaves

1 Cut ciabatta in half horizontally; reserve one half for another use. Remove and discard soft centre from remaining half; cut remaining bread into 2cm cubes.

2 Cut tomatoes into wedges; discard seeds, chop coarsely.

3 Cut celery into 4 strips lengthways; coarsely chop strips.

4 Peel cucumber; cut in half lengthways, discard seeds. Cut halves into 1cm-thick slices.

5 Chop onion coarsely, combine with bread cubes, tomato, celery and cucumber in large bowl.

6 Combine remaining ingredients for dressing in screw-top jar; shake well. Pour dressing over salad; toss gently.

SERVES 4

per serve 30.1g fat; 1600kJ

serving suggestion Serve with a glass of chianti for a light lunch or with your favourite Italian dish, such as veal scaloppine or baked sardines, for a delicious main meal.

tips Add capers for extra flavour.

• Instead of discarding the soft white centre of the bread, you can blend or process it into fine breadcrumbs, or try cutting it into small cubes and toasting until golden brown and crunchy.

Discarding soft centre of bread

Discarding tomato seeds

Chopping celery

seafood salad

PREPARATION TIME 50 MINUTES • COOKING TIME 15 MINUTES

500g baby octopus

2 large (500g) calamari hoods

1kg medium uncooked prawns

**1/4 cup finely chopped fresh
    flat-leaf parsley**

THOUSAND ISLAND DRESSING

1/2 cup (125ml) mayonnaise

1/2 cup (125ml) tomato puree

2 teaspoons Worcestershire sauce

1/4 teaspoon Tabasco sauce

**2 teaspoons capers,
    drained, chopped finely**

1 teaspoon Dijon mustard

2 hard-boiled eggs, grated finely

1 Remove and discard heads and beaks from octopus; cut each octopus in half.

2 Cut calamari lengthways down centre; lay out flat with inside facing upwards. Make shallow cuts diagonally across calamari; cut into 1cm slices in opposite direction.

3 Shell and devein prawns, leaving tails intact.

4 Working quickly, drop octopus and calamari into large pan of boiling water for 20 seconds; drain immediately.

5 Cook prawns and octopus, in batches, in heated oiled grill pan (or on grill or barbecue) until browned all over and cooked as desired.

6 Combine seafood and parsley in large bowl; toss gently. Serve seafood with dressing, and lettuce leaves, if desired.

thousand island dressing Whisk mayonnaise, puree, sauces, capers and mustard in small bowl until combined. Stir egg through dressing just before serving.

SERVES 4

per serve 16.2g fat; 1945kJ

serving suggestion This amount makes a healthy size first course seafood cocktail for six; otherwise, to serve four, accompany it with green salad.

tips Octopus heads *can* be used; remove eye section from head and discard. Peel skin from rest of head, rinse under cold water; dry with absorbent paper.

• Thousand island dressing can be made a day ahead and kept, covered, under refrigeration until needed.

Halving baby octopus

Scoring calamari and cutting into slices

Seeding olives

Slicing capsicum into rings

greek salad

PREPARATION TIME 25 MINUTES

Dried rigani, which resembles dried oregano but has longer leaves and is grey-green in colour, can be purchased in Greek and Middle-Eastern food shops.

4 medium (300g) egg tomatoes

2 (260g) Lebanese cucumbers

2 medium (400g) green capsicums

1 medium (170g) red onion

1 cup (160g) kalamata olives, seeded

150g Greek sheep milk fetta cheese

1 teaspoon crushed dried rigani

1/2 cup (125ml) extra virgin olive oil

1 Quarter tomatoes and cucumbers lengthways; cut into chunks. Slice capsicum into rings; remove and discard seeds and membranes. Cut onion into wedges.

2 Combine tomato, cucumber, capsicum, onion and olives in large serving bowl.

3 Break cheese into large pieces and place on top of salad, sprinkle with rigani; drizzle with oil.

SERVES 4

per serve 39.6g fat; 1779kJ

serving suggestion This salad is ideal with barbecued seafood (in Greece, barbecued octopus is usually served with it).
It's also good with grilled lamb skewers.

tips For an authentic Greek way of presenting this salad, leave the fetta in a whole piece and sit it on the top of the salad. Anchovies can be added to impart a salty flavour.

• Rigani is a type of oregano which grows wild in the mountains of Greece and tastes rather sharper than strong oregano; if you can't find it in your area, substitute a mixture of fresh or dried oregano and/or marjoram, but adjust the amount used to suit your taste.

DRIED RIGANI (WILD MARJORAM)

purees, dips and spreads

You can make these creamy salads by whisking them in a bowl or, for a smoother texture, you can use an electric blender or processor. Serve them as a first course with wedges of ciabatta, lavash, naan, pide, pitta or pocket pitta.

tahini salad

PREPARATION TIME 10 MINUTES

Tahini, a paste made from sesame seeds, is available from selected supermarkets and delicatessens.

3/4 cup (180ml) tahini

2 cloves garlic, crushed

1/4 cup (60ml) lemon juice

1/4 cup (60ml) water

1/4 teaspoon ground cumin

1 tablespoon finely chopped fresh parsley

1   Combine tahini and garlic in small bowl.

2   Gradually beat in juice, water, cumin and parsley, beating well until mixture thickens.

MAKES 1½ CUPS (350G)

per 100g 35g fat; 1526kJ

serving suggestion This Middle-Eastern cream salad is popular as a first course with pide bread or as an accompaniment to both hot and cold main dishes. Try it with sliced, toasted pide and crispy fried sardines.

guacamole

PREPARATION TIME 20 MINUTES

Guacamole is an avocado salad from Mexico, sometimes used as an accompaniment but best eaten on its own with corn chips. For extra flavour, try adding either crushed garlic, chopped green onion, finely chopped chilli or a few drops of Tabasco sauce.

1 medium (150g) white onion

2 small (260g) tomatoes

2 medium (500g) avocados

1 tablespoon lime juice

2 tablespoons coarsely chopped fresh coriander leaves

1   Chop onion and tomatoes finely.

2   Using a fork, mash avocados in medium bowl until almost smooth. Add onion, tomato, juice and coriander; mix well.

MAKES 3¼ CUPS (760G)

per 100g 10g fat; 433kJ

serving suggestion Serve guacamole with corn chips, salsa and sour cream. Also good with tacos, nachos and other Mexican dishes.

taramasalata

PREPARATION TIME 10 MINUTES

Taramasalata is a Greek "mayonnaise" made with tarama, the dried, salt-pressed and lightly smoked roe of the grey mullet. As this can be expensive, smoked cod's roe can be used instead. If you use genuine tarama you'll get an orange-coloured taramasalata, whereas with smoked cod's roe it is more rosy pink in colour. Taramasalata can be made a week ahead; keep, covered, in refrigerator.

4 slices stale white bread

100g can tarama

1 small (80g) brown onion, chopped coarsely

1 clove garlic, quartered

1/4 cup (60ml) lemon juice

11/2 cups (375ml) olive oil

1 Discard crusts from bread; soak bread in cold water for 2 minutes. Drain; squeeze water from bread with hands.

2 Blend or process bread, tarama, onion, garlic and juice until combined. With motor operating, add oil in thin stream; process until mixture thickens.

MAKES ABOUT 2 CUPS (670G)

per 100g 51.5g fat; 2111kJ

serving suggestion Serve as a dip, with wedges of ciabatta or pide and vegetable sticks, or as an accompaniment to fish kebabs.

cucumber, yogurt and mint salad

PREPARATION TIME 10 MINUTES
(plus standing time)

This Indian dish, called raita, is a great accompaniment to any hot curry; the refreshing flavour will cool the fiercest vindaloo! Salting the cucumber is essential to the recipe because the salt actually enhances the flavour.

3 large (1.2kg) green cucumbers

2 teaspoons coarse cooking salt

3/4 cup (180ml) yogurt

1 tablespoon finely chopped fresh mint leaves

1 clove garlic, crushed

1 Seed cucumbers; chop finely.

2 Place cucumber in colander, sprinkle with salt; stand 15 minutes. Rinse under cold water; drain on absorbent paper.

3 Combine yogurt, mint and garlic in medium bowl with cucumber; stir until combined.

MAKES 41/2 CUPS (940G)

per 100g 0.7g fat; 94kJ

serving suggestion Serve this refreshing salad as an accompaniment to any hot, spicy dish – particularly Indian curries – or serve it with crisp pappadums as a starter.

beetroot, cucumber and mint salad

PREPARATION TIME 25 MINUTES

A refreshing Middle-Eastern salad made with raw beetroot to give it a crunchy texture.

1 large (400g) green cucumber

1 teaspoon coarse cooking salt

4 medium (700g) fresh beetroot

1 medium (170g) red onion

2 tablespoons finely chopped fresh mint leaves

1 teaspoon finely grated lemon rind

1/2 cup (125ml) lemon juice

1 teaspoon sugar

1 Peel, seed and finely chop cucumber. Place cucumber in colander, sprinkle with salt; let mixture stand 15 minutes.

2 Meanwhile, peel and grate trimmed beetroot. Chop onion finely.

3 Rinse cucumber under cold water; drain on absorbent paper.

4 Combine cucumber, beetroot, onion, mint, rind, juice and sugar in large bowl.

MAKES 6 CUPS (1.25KG)

per 100g 0.1g fat; 133kJ

serving suggestion Serve with sliced char-grilled lamb fillet in pocket pittas with yogurt, or as an accompaniment to beef, lamb and game.

hummus

PREPARATION TIME 10 MINUTES (plus standing time)
• COOKING TIME 50 MINUTES

Hummus is a Middle-Eastern dip made with tahini, a sesame seed paste. You can buy tahini from selected supermarkets and delicatessens. If desired, 11/2 x 300g cans chickpeas, rinsed and drained, may be used instead of dried chickpeas. Hummus can be made 2 days ahead; keep, covered, in refrigerator.

3/4 cup (150g) dried chickpeas

1 teaspoon salt

1 clove garlic, quartered

1/3 cup (80ml) tahini

1/4 cup (60ml) lemon juice

pinch cayenne pepper

1 tablespoon coarsely chopped fresh flat-leaf parsley

1 Place chickpeas in medium bowl, cover with cold water; stand overnight.

2 Drain chickpeas, place in medium pan, cover with fresh water. Bring to boil; simmer, covered, about 50 minutes or until chickpeas are tender. Drain chickpeas over large heatproof bowl, discard as many skins as possible. Reserve 1/3 cup (80ml) chickpea liquid; discard remaining liquid.

3 Blend or process chickpeas with salt, garlic, tahini, juice and reserved liquid until almost smooth.

4 Spoon into serving bowl; sprinkle with pepper and parsley. Drizzle with 2 teaspoons olive oil, if desired.

MAKES 2 CUPS (550G)

per 100g 15g fat; 1005kJ (excludes oil for drizzling)

serving suggestion Serve with warm pide or toasted pitta, or as a sauce with grilled kebabs or roast lamb.

baba ghanoush

PREPARATION TIME 15 MINUTES (plus standing time)
• COOKING TIME 1 HOUR

Baba ghanoush is a Middle-Eastern puree of eggplant and tahini, which is usually served as a dip, but can be served as a salad by adding lots of black olives and tomato slices. If you find the smoky flavour too strong, soften it by stirring in one tablespoon of yogurt. Tahini, a sesame seed paste, is available from selected supermarkets and delicatessens.

2 large (1kg) eggplants
1/4 cup (60ml) tahini
1/4 cup (60ml) lemon juice
3 cloves garlic, quartered
1 teaspoon salt
2 tablespoons finely chopped fresh parsley

1 Pierce eggplants all over with fork or skewer; place whole eggplants on oiled oven tray. Bake, uncovered, in hot oven about 1 hour or until soft. Stand 15 minutes.

2 Peel eggplants, discard skins; chop flesh coarsely.

3 Blend or process eggplant with tahini, juice, garlic and salt, until combined. Spoon into serving bowl; sprinkle with parsley.

MAKES ABOUT 3 CUPS (700G)

per 100g 3.5g fat; 210kJ

serving suggestion Usually served as a dip with pitta bread, but it's also delicious as a sandwich spread or as an accompaniment to roast lamb.

moroccan carrot salad

PREPARATION TIME 15 MINUTES
• COOKING TIME 20 MINUTES

There are many versions of carrot salad in North Africa. This one calls for cooked carrots with a touch of spice, to add that authentic Moroccan flavour. Tahini, a paste made from sesame seeds, is available from selected supermarkets and delicatessens. This salad is best made a day ahead to allow the flavours to develop; keep, covered, in refrigerator.

10 medium (1.2kg) carrots
2 tablespoons olive oil
2 cloves garlic, crushed
1 tablespoon grated fresh ginger
2 teaspoons ground turmeric
1 teaspoon ground cumin
1 teaspoon ground cinnamon
2 tablespoons lemon juice
1/3 cup (80ml) tahini
1/3 cup (80ml) yogurt
2 tablespoons coarsely chopped fresh coriander leaves

1 Chop carrots coarsely; boil, steam or microwave until just tender, drain.

2 Heat the oil in large pan; cook garlic, ginger, turmeric, cumin and cinnamon until fragrant. Stir in juice and carrot; cook, stirring, until combined.

3 Remove from heat, stand 10 minutes; stir in tahini and yogurt. Process carrot mixture, in batches, until almost smooth. Just before serving, stir in coriander.

MAKES ABOUT 4 CUPS (1KG)

per 100g 7.2g fat; 401kJ

serving suggestion Serve with pitta, or as an accompaniment to char-grilled lamb or beef.

main meals

An incredible range of fresh ingredients now readily available in supermarkets means that,
in salads, you should expect the unexpected. Read on for some unique and appetising recipes

noodle wedges with smoked chicken

PREPARATION TIME 35 MINUTES (plus standing and refrigeration time) • COOKING TIME 15 MINUTES

You can substitute a purchased barbecued chicken for the smoked chicken if you like.

Cutting noodle cake into pieces

Slicing snow peas on the diagonal

Shredding smoked chicken

250g thin fresh egg noodles
1 tablespoon polenta
2 tablespoons olive oil
150g snow peas
150g green beans
4 green onions
400g coarsely shredded smoked chicken

THIN FRESH EGG NOODLES

LIME AND CHILLI DRESSING

1/2 cup (125ml) peanut oil
1/3 cup (80ml) lime juice
1 tablespoon sweet chilli sauce
1 tablespoon hoisin sauce

1 Place noodles in large heatproof bowl, cover with boiling water, stand 3 minutes; drain.

2 Sprinkle polenta over base of oiled deep 19cm-square cake pan. Press cooled noodles firmly into pan, cover; refrigerate 3 hours or overnight.

3 Turn noodle cake onto board; cut into quarters. Heat the oil in large pan; cook noodle squares, in batches, until browned lightly both sides. Drain on absorbent paper; cut each square into 2 triangles.

4 Slice snow peas diagonally; cut beans into 5cm lengths. Boil, steam or microwave snow peas and beans, separately, until just tender; drain. Cut onions into long thin strips.

5 Toss peas, beans and onion in large bowl with chicken. Divide noodle wedges among plates; top with chicken salad, drizzle with dressing.

lime and chilli dressing Combine ingredients in screw-top jar; shake well.

SERVES 4

per serve 48.8g fat; 3347kJ

tips Dressing can be made a day ahead and kept, covered, in refrigerator.

• Smoked chickens are very versatile – they can be used in a wide variety of dishes, from a salad to an omelette filling to a creamy pasta sauce.

Thinly slicing pork fillet

Trimming ends off curly endive

warm pork and mandarin salad

PREPARATION TIME 20 MINUTES (plus marinating time) • COOKING TIME 15 MINUTES

*Pork has a particular affinity with citrus flavours. If mandarins (also known as tangerines)
are out of season, try using their relative, the tangelo, in this recipe. You can also substitute
the fresh fruit for a drained 310g can of mandarin segments.*

500g pork fillet, sliced thinly

2 cloves garlic, crushed

1 teaspoon grated fresh ginger

1 tablespoon sweet chilli sauce

2 teaspoons soy sauce

**3 small (300g) mandarins,
  segmented**

150g sugar snap peas

2 tablespoons peanut oil

300g curly endive, trimmed

**1/4 cup firmly packed fresh
  coriander leaves**

**1 small (100g) red onion,
  sliced thinly**

CHILLI DRESSING

1 tablespoon white wine vinegar

1 tablespoon peanut oil

1 tablespoon sweet chilli sauce

2 teaspoons soy sauce

1 Combine pork, garlic, ginger and sauces in small bowl, cover;
   refrigerate 2 hours or overnight.

2 Halve mandarin segments lengthways; discard seeds.

3 Boil, steam or microwave peas until just tender; drain.

4 Heat the oil in wok or large pan; stir-fry pork, in batches,
   until browned and cooked as desired.

5 Gently toss pork, mandarin and peas in large bowl with endive,
   coriander, onion and dressing.

chilli dressing Combine ingredients in screw-top jar; shake well.

SERVES 4

per serve 25g fat; 1630kJ

SUGAR SNAP PEAS

warm salad of scampi with wonton crisps

PREPARATION TIME 35 MINUTES • COOKING TIME 10 MINUTES

You can use gow-gee or spring-roll wrappers in place of the wonton wrappers.

peanut oil, for deep-frying

8 wonton wrappers

2 Dutch red chillies, seeded, sliced thinly

1 tablespoon finely chopped fresh lemon grass

1/4 cup (55g) sugar

1/3 cup (80ml) water

1kg cooked scampi

1 medium (200g) red capsicum, sliced thinly

1 medium (200g) yellow capsicum, sliced thinly

1 medium (200g) green capsicum, sliced thinly

2 tablespoons coarsely chopped fresh coriander leaves

1 Heat the oil in medium pan or wok; deep-fry wonton wrappers, in batches, until lightly browned and crisp. Drain on absorbent paper.

2 Combine chilli, lemon grass, sugar and the water in medium pan; stir over heat, without boiling, until sugar dissolves. Bring to boil, simmer, uncovered, about 5 minutes or until dressing thickens slightly.

3 Meanwhile, shell and devein scampi.

4 Gently toss scampi in large heatproof bowl with capsicums, coriander and warm dressing; serve salad with wonton crisps.

SCAMPI

SERVES 4

per serve 2.3g fat; 915kJ (excludes oil for deep-frying)

tip Scampi is the Italian name for the sweet-tasting seawater shellfish that look like giant prawns; in restaurant cooking, this term is also used to describe a certain way of butterflying and grilling very big prawns. You can make use of the discarded shells by cooking them in a pan of boiling water until liquid has reduced to the concentrated stock, called a fumet, used to make seafood reduction sauces.

Deep-frying whole wonton wrappers

Discarding seeds from the chillies

chicken salad

PREPARATION TIME 30 MINUTES • COOKING TIME 10 MINUTES

When you're short on time, instead of poaching fresh chicken buy two cooked chickens and use their meat in this recipe.

2 egg yolks

2 tablespoons lemon juice

1 tablespoon Dijon mustard

1/2 cup (125ml) vegetable oil

1/2 cup (125ml) light olive oil

5 cups (750g) coarsely chopped cooked chicken

5 trimmed (375g) celery sticks, sliced thinly

1/2 cup (70g) slivered almonds, toasted

4 hard-boiled eggs, quartered

1 Blend or process egg yolks, juice and mustard until smooth.

2 With motor operating, gradually pour in combined oils; process until mayonnaise thickens.

3 Gently toss chicken, celery, almonds and hard-boiled egg in large bowl with mayonnaise. Serve salad spooned into lettuce leaves with crusty bread, if desired.

SERVES 6

per serve 58.7g fat; 2794kJ

tips To centre yolks, place eggs in pan of cold water, gently stir until water boils; cook, uncovered, stirring occasionally, about 6 minutes or until hard-boiled.

• To toast slivered almonds, place nuts on ungreased oven tray; bake in moderate oven, uncovered, about 5 minutes or until lightly browned.

Toasting slivered almonds

Stirring eggs to centre yolks

thai-style vegetarian salad

PREPARATION TIME 30 MINUTES • COOKING TIME 15 MINUTES

*This is a vegetarian take on that wonderful Thai noodle dish usually containing prawns,
and sometimes pork or chicken, called Phad Thai.*

375g rice stick noodles

4 eggs

**2 tablespoons finely
  chopped fresh chives**

1 teaspoon peanut oil

300g fresh tofu

vegetable oil, for deep-frying

1 (130g) Lebanese cucumber

250g bean sprouts

**2 tablespoons finely chopped
  fresh lemon grass**

2 red Thai chillies, sliced thinly

**1 tablespoon finely chopped
  fresh coriander leaves**

**3/4 cup (110g) coarsely chopped
  roasted unsalted peanuts**

3 green onions, sliced finely

CHILLI SOY DRESSING

2 tablespoons sweet chilli sauce

2 tablespoons soy sauce

2 cloves garlic, crushed

1 tablespoon brown sugar

1 tablespoon tomato sauce

2 teaspoons fish sauce

2 tablespoons peanut oil

1 Place noodles in large heatproof bowl, cover with boiling water, let
  stand about 10 minutes or until softened; drain.

2 Meanwhile, whisk eggs and chives together in medium bowl. Heat half
  the peanut oil in wok or large pan; add half the egg mixture, swirl wok
  so egg forms a thin omelette over base, cook until set. Remove from
  wok; cool. Repeat with remaining peanut oil and egg mixture. Roll
  omelettes firmly; cut into thin slices.

3 Cut tofu into 2cm cubes. Heat vegetable oil in medium pan; deep-fry
  tofu, in batches, until golden brown. Drain on absorbent paper.

4 Halve cucumber lengthways; discard seeds. Slice cucumber thinly on
  the diagonal. Snap ends off bean sprouts.

5 Gently toss noodles, omelette, tofu, cucumber and sprouts in large
  bowl with remaining ingredients and dressing.

chilli soy dressing Combine ingredients in screw-top jar; shake well.

SERVES 4

per serve 36.8g fat; 3015kJ (excludes oil for deep-frying)

Slicing rolled omelette into thin wheels

Chopping the green vegetables

Thinly slicing barbecued pork

wilted chinese greens, pork and tofu with macadamia dressing

PREPARATION TIME 30 MINUTES • COOKING TIME 10 MINUTES

Ready-to-eat barbecued pork can be purchased from specialty Asian food stores.

500g choy sum
350g Chinese broccoli
500g baby bok choy
4 green onions
2 tablespoons peanut oil
200g fresh shiitake
 mushrooms, quartered
500g Chinese barbecued
 pork, sliced thinly
300g fresh tofu, cubed
1 cup (100g) mung bean sprouts

MACADAMIA DRESSING

1/2 cup macadamias,
 toasted, chopped finely
1/2 cup (125ml) peanut oil
1/4 cup (60ml) mirin
1 tablespoon soy sauce
1/3 cup (80ml) rice vinegar

1 Trim green vegetables; chop coarsely. Cut onions into 5cm lengths.

2 Heat half of the oil in wok or large pan; stir-fry onion and mushroom until mushrooms are just tender. Add pork, stir-fry 1 minute; remove mixture from wok.

3 Heat remaining oil in same wok; stir-fry choy sum, broccoli and bok choy until just wilted.

4 Gently toss pork mixture, vegetable mixture, tofu and sprouts in large bowl with dressing.

macadamia dressing Combine ingredients in screw-top jar; shake well.

SERVES 4

per serve 77.1g fat; 3797kJ

FRESH SHIITAKE MUSHROOMS

soba and tuna salad

PREPARATION TIME 15 MINUTES • COOKING TIME 10 MINUTES

Yellowfin tuna, also known as ahi, can weigh up to 135kg; its flesh is a deep pink colour and has a rich, strong flavour. While it is prized in Japanese dishes like sashimi and sushi, it is generally eaten raw – as is the case in this recipe. If you prefer your tuna cooked, pan-fry it until crisp on the outside and cooked as you like within, then proceed with this recipe. We suggest you check local regulations before eating any raw seafood.

500g soba

1 medium (120g) carrot

50g pickled daikon, sliced thinly

**2 tablespoons drained
    pickled ginger slices**

**500g fresh yellowfin tuna,
    sliced thinly**

**1 sheet toasted nori,
    shredded thinly**

2 tablespoons soy sauce

2 tablespoons mirin

1 teaspoon wasabi

1 Cook soba in large pan of boiling water, uncovered, until just tender; drain. Rinse under cold water; drain, pat dry with absorbent paper.

2 Using vegetable peeler, cut carrot into long thin ribbons.

3 Cut daikon into thin slices, then into matchstick-size pieces.

4 Place soba, carrot, daikon, ginger and tuna on serving plates, sprinkle salad with nori.

5 Whisk soy sauce, mirin and wasabi in small bowl; drizzle over salad.

SERVES 4

per serve 3.8g fat; 1470kJ

tip This delicious recipe is almost a lesson in Japanese cooking since it features many of that country's most commonly used ingredients. Nori is sold as thin sheets of dried seaweed, used whole in sushi-making or shredded as a garnish for soups, salads and stews. Daikon is a huge, carrot-shaped white radish, often eaten raw but also sold in dried and pickled forms. Soba is a spaghetti-thin Japanese noodle made of buckwheat flour and varying proportions of wheat flour. Wasabi, Japanese horseradish, is sold in powdered or paste form; make up the powder following package directions. Increase the amount of wasabi in the dressing recipe for more bite. Mirin is an ale-coloured, slightly sweet cooking wine made from glutinous rice – it is not a wine made to be quaffed!

SOBA

Cutting carrot into long, thin ribbons

Thinly slicing pickled daikon

Shredding toasted nori

tandoori beef and dhal with cucumber dressing

PREPARATION TIME 25 MINUTES (plus marinating time) • COOKING TIME 35 MINUTES (plus resting time)

Pale-yellow moong dhal is what we commonly call split mung beans, red lentils can be used instead, if desired, we didn't read the chillies deliberately in this recipe, but do so by all means if you can't stand the heat!

2 teaspoons ground turmeric

2 teaspoons ground cumin

2 teaspoons ground coriander

1 tablespoon sweet paprika

1 teaspoon garlic salt

1/4 cup (60ml) peanut oil

800g beef fillet

1 cup (200g) moong dhal

150g green beans

2 red Thai chillies, sliced thinly

1 medium (170g) red onion, chopped finely

1 tablespoon cumin seeds, toasted

CUCUMBER DRESSING

1 (130g) Lebanese cucumber

200ml yogurt

1/2 cup loosely packed fresh mint leaves

1 tablespoon lemon juice

1 Combine spices, salt and the oil in large bowl. Add beef, coat with spice mixture, cover; refrigerate 3 hours or overnight.

2 Cook beef in heated large non-stick pan, uncovered, about 5 minutes or until browned all over. Place beef in baking dish; bake, uncovered, in moderate oven about 30 minutes or until cooked as desired. Cover beef; rest 10 minutes, slice thinly.

3 Meanwhile, add dhal to pan of boiling water; cook, uncovered, about 10 minutes or until just tender, stirring occasionally. Drain, cool.

4 Top and tail beans; cut into 3cm lengths. Boil, steam or microwave beans until just tender; rinse under cold water, drain.

5 Gently toss beef, dhal, beans, chilli, onion and seeds in large bowl with dressing.

cucumber dressing Cut cucumber in half lengthways, discard seeds; chop coarsely. Blend or process cucumber and remaining ingredients until almost smooth.

SERVES 4

per serve 27.3g fat; 2302kJ

tips To toast cumin seeds, dry-fry in small pan, stirring until fragrant.

• Dressing is best if made at least 3 hours ahead; keep, covered, in refrigerator.

MOONG DHAL

Removing seeds from cucumber

Cooking onion, garlic and tomato

Cooking haloumi

haloumi, olive and tomato salad

PREPARATION TIME 30 MINUTES • COOKING TIME 10 MINUTES

Substitute fresh rocket leaves for baby spinach leaves, if desired. If teardrop tomatoes are particularly large, halve them before cooking.

2 tablespoons olive oil

1 large (200g) brown onion, sliced

2 cloves garlic, crushed

250g cherry tomatoes, halved

250g yellow teardrop tomatoes

500g haloumi cheese, sliced thickly

1/4 cup finely chopped fresh parsley

1/2 cup (60g) seeded black olives

200g baby spinach leaves

1/4 cup (60ml) lemon juice

1 Heat half of the oil in large pan; cook onion and garlic, stirring, until onion is just browned. Add tomatoes; cook, stirring, until just soft. Cover to keep warm.

2 Heat remaining oil in large pan; cook cheese, in batches, until browned both sides. Drain on absorbent paper.

3 Gently toss cheese and tomato mixture in large bowl with parsley, olives, spinach and juice.

SERVES 4

per serve 15.9g fat; 915kJ

tip Haloumi must be cooked just before serving; fry it any sooner and it can become rather leathery and unpalatable.

HALOUMI CHEESE

chef's salad

PREPARATION TIME 20 MINUTES (plus cooling time) • COOKING TIME 25 MINUTES

This ubiquitous American favourite can be found on hotel room-service menus everywhere in the world. Once you make it yourself at home, you'll understand why! With a loaf of fresh bread, it's a meal in itself.

350g chicken breast fillets

3 medium (225g) egg tomatoes

1 large cos lettuce

200g finely sliced leg ham

100g finely sliced
   Jarlsberg cheese

3 hard-boiled eggs, quartered

VINAIGRETTE

1/2 cup (125ml) olive oil

1/4 cup (60ml) white wine vinegar

2 teaspoons seeded mustard

1 teaspoon sugar

1/4 teaspoon cracked pepper

1 Cook chicken in heated oiled large pan until browned both sides.

2 Place chicken in shallow baking dish; bake, uncovered, in moderate oven about 15 minutes or until cooked through. Cool 5 minutes; cut into thin slices.

3 Cut each tomato into 8 wedges. Wash and separate lettuce leaves; tear into small pieces.

JARLSBERG CHEESE

4 Divide lettuce among serving bowls; layer with chicken, tomato, ham, cheese and egg, then drizzle with vinaigrette.

vinaigrette Combine ingredients in screw-top jar; shake well.

SERVES 4

per serve 48.2g fat; 2737kJ

tips Gruyère or Emmenthaler can be used in place of the Jarlsberg cheese, and prosciutto substitutes wonderfully for the leg ham.

• This dressing is a classic vinaigrette. To make it even creamier, place ingredients in a blender and process until thick and opaque. You can prepare the vinaigrette a day ahead; keep it, covered, in the refrigerator.

Cutting tomatoes into wedges

Tearing the lettuce

Cutting polenta mixture into rounds

crisp polenta and vegetable salad

PREPARATION TIME 15 MINUTES (plus refrigerating time) • COOKING TIME 40 MINUTES

Used by people the world over, polenta is a versatile product made from dried, ground corn. North Americans use it as the basis for porridge-like mush; it is also used in Mexican tortillas; and Italians use it in sweet cakes, or eat it baked then fried.

2 cups (500ml) vegetable stock
3 cups (750ml) water
3 cups (510g) polenta
2/3 cup (50g) coarsely grated
  parmesan cheese
200g fetta cheese, crumbled
1/3 cup finely shredded
  fresh basil leaves
2 medium (400g)
  yellow capsicums
2 medium (240g) zucchini
1 small (230g) eggplant
1 large (250g) tomato, sliced
50g baby spinach leaves

WARM TOMATO DRESSING

170ml can tomato juice
1 tablespoon balsamic vinegar
1 clove garlic, crushed
2 tablespoons finely shredded
  fresh basil leaves

1 Bring stock and the water to boil in large pan; gradually stir in polenta. Simmer, stirring, about 5 minutes or until mixture thickens; stir in cheeses and basil. Press polenta mixture into two oiled 23cm-square cake pans, cover; refrigerate about 3 hours or until firm.

2 Quarter capsicums, remove and discard seeds and membranes. Roast under grill or in very hot oven, skin-side up, until skin blisters and blackens. Cover capsicum pieces in plastic or paper for 5 minutes; peel away skin.

3 Turn polenta mixture onto board; using 7.5cm cutter, cut into 12 rounds.

4 Cook polenta rounds, in batches, on heated oiled grill plate (or grill or barbecue) until browned both sides and heated through; cover to keep warm.

5 Cut zucchini lengthways into thin slices. Cut eggplant into 1cm-thick rounds. Cook zucchini, in batches, on heated oiled grill plate (or grill or barbecue) until browned both sides and just tender. Repeat with eggplant and tomato.

6 Divide polenta, capsicum, zucchini, eggplant, tomato and spinach among serving plates; drizzle with dressing.

warm tomato dressing Combine ingredients in small pan; stir over heat until warm.

SERVES 6

per serve 12.7g fat; 1923kJ

POLENTA

Halving snow peas

Slicing seeded telegraph cucumber

beef and rice vermicelli salad with lime and chilli dressing

PREPARATION TIME 10 MINUTES • COOKING TIME 10 MINUTES

400g beef rump steak
100g rice vermicelli
150g snow peas
1 (400g) telegraph cucumber
1 tablespoon fresh
  coriander leaves

LIME AND CHILLI DRESSING

¼ cup (60ml) lime juice
2 tablespoons peanut oil
1 red Thai chilli, seeded, sliced

1 Cook beef on heated oiled grill plate (or grill or barbecue) until browned both sides and cooked as desired. Cover; rest 5 minutes, slice thinly.

2 Meanwhile, cook vermicelli in large pan of boiling water, uncovered, about 2 minutes or until just tender; drain. Rinse vermicelli under cold water; drain.

3 Slice snow peas in half diagonally. Cut cucumber in half lengthways; discard seeds, slice diagonally.

4 Gently toss beef, vermicelli, peas and cucumber in large bowl with dressing; sprinkle with coriander leaves.

lime and chilli dressing
Combine ingredients in screw-top jar; shake well.

SERVES 4

per serve 16.6g fat; 1333kJ

RICE VERMICELLI

insalata di mare

PREPARATION TIME 40 MINUTES (plus refrigeration time) • COOKING TIME 20 MINUTES

Insalata di mare is found in Italian restaurants around the world. Great as a meal with a simple green salad and a loaf of fresh ciabatta, you'll want to serve this again and again.

600g medium uncooked prawns

750g mussels

1/3 cup (80ml) olive oil

1 clove garlic, crushed

**500g cleaned baby
    octopus, quartered**

400g calamari rings

1 cup (250ml) dry white wine

750g clams

2 cloves garlic, crushed, extra

**1/2 cup coarsely chopped
    fresh flat-leaf parsley**

1/3 cup (80ml) lemon juice

1 Shell and devein prawns, leaving tails intact. Scrub mussels; remove beards.

2 Heat 1 tablespoon of the oil in medium pan; cook garlic and prawns, in batches, until prawns are just changed in colour.

MUSSELS (BLACK SHELLS) AND CLAMS

3 Cook octopus and calamari, in batches, in same pan until cooked through.

4 Bring wine to boil in same pan; simmer, uncovered, until reduced by half. Add mussels and clams; cook, covered, until shells open (discard any that do not open).

5 Combine remaining oil with extra garlic, parsley and juice in screw-top jar; shake well. Combine dressing with prawns, mussels, octopus, calamari and clams in large bowl, cover; refrigerate 1 hour. Gently toss salad again just before serving.

SERVES 4

per serve 21.2g fat; 1435kJ

tip This salad is best prepared close to serving time, but do allow for the one hour of refrigeration to allow the flavours to develop.

De-bearding the mussels

Cutting the baby octopus into quarters

smoked salmon and caviar salad

PREPARATION TIME 15 MINUTES • COOKING TIME 30 MINUTES

A luxury dish for that special occasion, this recipe is made more affordable by the inclusion of red caviar (lightly salted salmon roe) in preference to its more expensive cousin, beluga caviar (lightly salted sturgeon roe). If you feel so inclined, you can substitute beluga caviar for the red caviar and accompany it with Champagne – French, of course!

1.2kg kipfler potatoes
1 tablespoon olive oil
500g fresh asparagus, trimmed
400g finely sliced smoked salmon
100g mesclun
25g red caviar

AVOCADO PUREE

1 small (200g) avocado
1/4 cup (60ml) sour cream
1 tablespoon finely chopped
** fresh dill**
2 tablespoons lime juice

RED CAVIAR

1 Boil, steam or microwave potatoes until just tender; drain.

2 Halve potatoes; place, cut-side up, on lightly oiled oven tray, drizzle with the oil. Bake, uncovered, in very hot oven about 15 minutes or until crisp and brown, turning occasionally.

3 Boil, steam or microwave asparagus until just tender; drain, cut spears in half crossways.

4 Cut salmon slices into strips.

5 Divide avocado puree among serving plates; top with potato, mesclun, asparagus, salmon and caviar.

avocado puree Halve avocado; discard stone, chop flesh coarsely. Blend or process avocado with remaining ingredients until smooth.

SERVES 4

per serve 24.2g fat; 2216kJ

tip Kipflers are small, bumpy, finger-shaped potatoes with a nutty flavour; they are particularly well-suited for salads that contain oven-roasted potatoes.

Halving the kipfler potatoes lengthways

Processing the avocado puree

mexican prawn salad

PREPARATION TIME 20 MINUTES (plus soaking and cooling time) • COOKING TIME 20 MINUTES

We used dried kidney beans in this recipe but, if you're in a rush, you can substitute a 420g can of kidney beans, rinsed and drained. The chillies are the kind found bottled in vinegar or olive oil in Mexican, Middle-Eastern or Italian food stores – long and sweet with just a bit of heat – perfect munched on with other pre-dinner snacks!

1 cup (200g) dried kidney beans

750g medium cooked prawns

1 (400g) fresh corn cob

4 corn tortillas

250g cherry tomatoes, halved

1 large (320g) avocado,
  sliced thinly

1 medium (170g) red onion,
  sliced finely

1/4 cup firmly packed fresh
  coriander leaves

2 pickled green chillies,
  drained, chopped coarsely

LIME DRESSING

1/4 cup (60ml) lime juice

2 teaspoons cumin seeds, toasted

1 red Thai chilli, seeded,
  chopped finely

1/3 cup (80ml) peanut oil

1 Cover beans with cold water in large bowl; soak overnight.

2 Drain beans, place in large pan of boiling water. Cook, uncovered, about 20 minutes or until just tender; drain, cool.

3 Meanwhile, shell and devein prawns, leaving tails intact.

4 Remove husk and silk from corn. Cut corn into 2cm-thick rounds; cut rounds in half. Boil, steam or microwave corn until tender; drain.

5 Cut each tortilla into eight pieces; place, in single layer, on oiled oven tray. Bake in moderate oven, uncovered, about 5 minutes or until browned lightly and crisp.

6 Gently toss beans, prawns, corn, tomato, avocado, onion, coriander and chilli in large bowl with dressing; serve salad with tortilla crisps.

lime dressing Combine ingredients in screw-top jar; shake well.

SERVES 4

per serve 21.7g fat; 1912kJ

tip Corn tortillas are sold fresh under refrigeration, frozen, or cryovac-packed on supermarket shelves. Keep some on hand to use as wrappers for leftover meatloaf, bolognese sauce or even grilled sausages. Make certain you get corn tortillas for this recipe – not the flour variety.

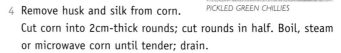
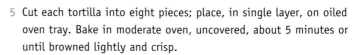

PICKLED GREEN CHILLIES

Cutting each tortilla into eight pieces

iskender kebab salad

PREPARATION TIME 20 MINUTES (plus marinating and standing time) • COOKING TIME 15 MINUTES

Iskender kebab, also known as yogurtlu kebab, is a classic dish from the region surrounding the Turkish capital of Ankara, where it is sold by weight in some of the many restaurants dedicated to its preparation. Turkish restaurants in this country also have it on the menu – it's so delicious you may find yourself ordering large portions! Here, we've adapted it into salad form.

750g lamb fillets
1 tablespoon finely grated
   lemon rind
2 cloves garlic, crushed
1/4 cup olive oil
1 long loaf pide
2 (260g) Lebanese cucumbers
2 medium (380g) tomatoes, seeded
1 medium (170g) red onion,
   chopped finely

2 red Thai chillies, seeded,
   chopped finely
1/3 cup loosely packed
   fresh flat-leaf parsley
1/4 cup loosely packed chopped
   fresh mint leaves

YOGURT DRESSING

1 tablespoon lemon juice
1 clove garlic, crushed
200ml yogurt

1 Combine lamb, rind, garlic and 2 tablespoons of the oil in large bowl, cover; refrigerate 3 hours or overnight.

2 Halve pide crossways; cut half into 2cm cubes, reserve remaining half for another use. Place pide cubes in large baking dish, drizzle with remaining oil; bake, uncovered, in hot oven, stirring occasionally, about 10 minutes or until browned all over and crisp.

3 Meanwhile, cook lamb, in batches, on heated oiled grill plate (or grill or barbecue) until browned all over and cooked as desired. Cover; rest 5 minutes, slice thinly.

4 Cut cucumbers and tomatoes in even-sized pieces.

5 Gently toss lamb, pide, cucumber and tomato in large bowl with onion, chilli and herbs; drizzle with dressing.

yogurt dressing Whisk ingredients in small bowl.

SERVES 4

per serve 32.3g fat; 2500kJ

tip This is another salad that "travels" well: pack the yogurt dressing and pide croutons separately to the assembled salad and toss when you get to the site of your meal. The dressing and croutons can be made a day ahead. Keep the dressing, covered, under refrigeration and the croutons airtight.

Thinly slicing chicken

Cutting green onion into strips

caramelised chicken noodle salad

PREPARATION TIME 20 MINUTES (plus standing time) • COOKING TIME 20 MINUTES

Palm sugar can be substituted with ¹/₄ cup brown sugar, if necessary.

65g palm sugar

1 clove garlic, crushed

1 tablespoon lime juice

1 teaspoon fish sauce

2 teaspoons sambal oelek

750g chicken tenderloins

6 green onions

1 large (180g) carrot

2 small (300g) green capsicums

420g fresh egg noodles

INDONESIAN DRESSING

2 tablespoons peanut oil

2 tablespoons lime juice

2 tablespoons sweet chilli sauce

1 tablespoon fish sauce

1 Cook sugar, garlic, juice, sauce and sambal in large pan, stirring, over low heat until sugar dissolves. Simmer, uncovered, about 3 minutes or until mixture starts to caramelise.

2 Add chicken to pan; cook over low heat, uncovered, until chicken is caramelised and cooked through, turning occasionally. Remove from pan, cool 10 minutes; slice thinly.

3 Meanwhile, cut onions into 5cm lengths; cut lengths into thin strips. Cut carrot into 2mm-wide lengths; cut lengths into thin strips. Quarter capsicums, remove seeds and membranes; cut capsicum into thin strips. Boil, steam or microwave carrot and capsicum, separately, until just tender; drain.

4 Place noodles in large heatproof bowl, cover with boiling water, stand 5 minutes; drain.

5 Combine noodles, chicken, onion, carrot and capsicum in large bowl with dressing.

indonesian dressing Combine ingredients in screw-top jar; shake well.

SERVES 4

per serve 18.5g fat; 2319kJ

cobb salad

PREPARATION TIME 30 MINUTES (plus cooling time) • COOKING TIME 20 MINUTES

The now-famous Cobb Salad was created by Robert Cobb at Hollywood's Brown Derby Restaurant during the 1930s.

1/2 cup (125ml) dry white wine

3 cups (750ml) water

1 tablespoon finely chopped
  fresh thyme leaves

700g chicken breast fillets

6 bacon rashers, chopped coarsely

4 hard-boiled eggs

1 small red oak leaf lettuce

100g watercress, trimmed

2 medium (500g) avocados,
  chopped coarsely

4 medium (760g) tomatoes,
  peeled, seeded, chopped coarsely

200g blue cheese

GARLIC VINAIGRETTE

1/4 cup (60ml) white wine vinegar

2 tablespoons light olive oil

1 teaspoon Dijon mustard

1 clove garlic, crushed

1 Combine wine, the water and thyme in large pan with chicken; bring to boil. Simmer, covered, about 20 minutes or until chicken is cooked through. Drain chicken; reserve poaching liquid for another use, if desired. When chicken is cool enough to handle, chop coarsely.

2 Meanwhile, cook bacon, stirring, in heated medium pan until browned and crisp; drain on absorbent paper.

3 Shell eggs, separate yolks and whites; chop egg whites coarsely, push yolks through fine sieve.

4 Divide lettuce and watercress among serving plates, top with chicken, bacon, egg white, egg yolk, avocado, tomato and crumbled cheese; drizzle salad with vinaigrette.

garlic vinaigrette Combine ingredients in screw-top jar; shake well.

SERVES 4

per serve 70.7g fat; 4076kJ

tip Leftover roast turkey, minus the skin and bones, can be substituted for the chicken.

WATERCRESS

Pushing egg yolks through sieve

Crumbling blue cheese over salad

salmon and pasta salad with dill dressing

PREPARATION TIME 15 MINUTES

We cooked a 375g packet of dried small pasta shells for this recipe. Cornichons, sold in bottles or loose (by weight) in delicatessens, are the tiny pickled gherkins served with pâté in French restaurants. Use any sweet baby pickled gherkins if you cannot locate cornichons.

2 x 415g cans red salmon, drained
2 bulbs (340g) baby fennel,
 sliced thinly
750g cooked small pasta shells
1 large (300g) red onion,
 chopped finely
350g cornichons, drained, halved
1 tablespoon finely
 chopped capers

DILL DRESSING

¹/₃ cup finely chopped fresh dill
¹/₂ cup (125ml) white
 wine vinegar
¹/₂ cup (125ml) lemon juice
²/₃ cup (160ml) olive oil
1 tablespoon seeded mustard

1 Remove any bones from drained salmon; flake salmon with a fork.

2 Gently toss salmon, fennel, pasta, onion, cornichon and capers in large bowl with dressing.

dill dressing Combine ingredients in screw-top jar; shake well.

SERVES 4

per serve 57g fat; 4073kJ

CORNICHONS

Thinly slicing baby fennel

Removing bones from salmon

Caramelising the apple wedges

Thinly slicing nashi

witlof and nashi salad

PREPARATION TIME 35 MINUTES • COOKING TIME 15 MINUTES

A soft herb-flavoured cheese such as Rondele can be substituted for the blue cheese in this recipe. We used Granny Smith apples for their pleasant tartness.

3 pieces lavash

150g blue cheese

1/2 cup (125ml) buttermilk

2 tablespoons milk

2 medium (300g) apples

20g butter

2 teaspoons brown sugar

2 medium (400g) nashi

500g witlof, leaves separated

2 small green oak leaf lettuces

1 cup (100g) pecans, toasted

1 Cut lavash into 3cm-wide strips. Place on ungreased oven tray; bake, uncovered, in moderate oven about 8 minutes or until crisp.

2 Meanwhile, blend or process cheese, buttermilk and milk until smooth. Place buttermilk dressing in small bowl,; cover surface with plastic wrap to prevent skin forming.

3 Cut cored apples into quarters, cut each quarter in half. Heat butter and sugar in medium pan; cook apple, turning occasionally, until coated all over with caramel mixture.

4 Cut nashi into quarters; slice thinly.

5 Divide lavash among serving plates, top with witlof and lettuce leaves, apple, nashi and nuts; drizzle with dressing.

SERVES 4

per serve 37.5g fat; 2802kJ

tips Nashi is a Japanese fruit somewhat like a cross between a pear and an apple; substitute corella pears if nashi are not available.

• Lavash and nuts can be prepared a day ahead and kept, separately, in airtight containers.

NASHI

Roasting capsicum before peeling

moroccan chicken salad

PREPARATION TIME 30 MINUTES (plus marinating and standing time) • COOKING TIME 40 MINUTES

1 tablespoon Moroccan Spice Mix

2 tablespoons olive oil

350g chicken breast fillets

1 medium (300g) eggplant

coarse cooking salt

2 large (700g) red capsicums

2 cups (500ml) water

2 cups (400g) couscous

1/2 cup (75g) shelled
pistachios, toasted

1/4 cup firmly packed fresh
coriander leaves

1/4 cup firmly packed fresh
mint leaves

MOROCCAN DRESSING

1/2 cup (125ml) lemon juice

1 tablespoon finely shredded
lemon rind

1/3 cup (80ml) olive oil

2 cloves garlic, crushed

8 cardamom pods, bruised

1 teaspoon cumin seeds, toasted

1/2 teaspoon ground turmeric

1 Combine Spice Mix and 1 tablespoon of the oil in large bowl. Add chicken, coat with spice mixture, cover; refrigerate 30 minutes.

2 Meanwhile, chop unpeeled eggplant into 2cm cubes, sprinkle all over with salt; stand 20 minutes.

3 Quarter capsicums, remove and discard seeds and membranes. Roast under grill or in very hot oven, skin-side up, until skin blisters and blackens. Cover capsicum pieces in plastic or paper for 5 minutes, peel away skin; chop capsicum coarsely.

4 Cook chicken, in batches, in heated oiled large pan, until browned all over and cooked through. Cover chicken; rest 5 minutes, slice thinly.

5 Rinse eggplant thoroughly under cold water; drain. Pat dry with absorbent paper. Heat remaining oil in same pan; cook eggplant, in batches, stirring, until browned all over and tender.

6 Bring the water to boil in medium pan; gradually add couscous, remove from heat. Cover, stand about 5 minutes or until all water is absorbed; fluff with fork.

7 Gently toss chicken, eggplant, capsicum, couscous, nuts, coriander and mint in large bowl with dressing.

moroccan dressing Combine ingredients in screw-top jar; shake well.

SERVES 4

per serve 42.5g fat; 2651kJ

tip To bruise cardamom, press down on pod with the side of a heavy knife or cleaver until pod is just crushed. If using in a cooked dish such as Middle-Eastern pilaf or a curry, use both pods and seeds while cooking; then discard pods before serving.

seared crab and rice ball salad

PREPARATION TIME 20 MINUTES (plus refrigeration time) • COOKING TIME 10 MINUTES

Koshihikari rice, a small, round, white grain, is available at most supermarkets. If unavailable, use white short-grain rice and cook by the absorption method. You need 1 cup of uncooked rice for this recipe.

3 cups cooked koshihikari rice

1 tablespoon rice vinegar

1 teaspoon sugar

170g can crab meat

1 clove garlic, crushed

1 tablespoon finely chopped
  fresh lemon grass

2 teaspoons grated fresh ginger

2 red Thai chillies, seeded,
  chopped finely

2 green onions, chopped finely

1 tablespoon kalonji

vegetable oil, for deep-frying

200g red radishes

300g mizuna

HORSERADISH DRESSING

2 teaspoons horseradish cream

1/2 cup (125ml) olive oil

2 tablespoons lemon juice

2 teaspoons sugar

1/3 cup (80ml) cider vinegar

2 tablespoons chopped fresh dill

1 teaspoon wasabi

1 Combine rice, vinegar and sugar in medium bowl, cover; refrigerate about 30 minutes or until rice is cold and sticky.

2 Drain crab; remove any shell remnants. Press crab to extract excess liquid.

3 Stir crab, garlic, lemon grass, ginger, chilli, onion and kalonji into rice mixture. Using wet hands, roll level tablespoons of rice mixture into balls.

4 Deep-fry rice balls, in batches, in hot oil until browned and crisp; drain on absorbent paper.

5 Slice radishes into 5mm-thick rounds; cut each round into 5mm-thick sticks. Gently toss radish and mizuna in large bowl with half of the dressing; serve salad with rice balls. Place remaining dressing in small bowl as dipping sauce.

horseradish dressing Combine horseradish, oil, juice and sugar in small bowl; whisk in vinegar, dill and wasabi.

SERVES 4

per serve 30.6g fat; 2137kJ (excludes oil for deep-frying)

tips Kalonji seeds, also known as black onion seeds or nigella, are found sprinkled over Turkish pide or in many Indian curries – they have a particularly enlivening taste.

• Wasabi, Japanese horseradish, is sold in powdered or paste form; make up the powder following package directions. Increase the amount of wasabi in this recipe for more bite.

KALONJI

Pressing on crab to extract liquid

soy chicken and green-onion omelette salad

PREPARATION TIME 20 MINUTES (plus marinating time) • COOKING TIME 25 MINUTES

700g chicken breast fillets
2 tablespoons soy sauce
1 clove garlic, crushed
1 tablespoon peanut oil
6 eggs
4 green onions, sliced thinly
50g tat soi leaves
50g snow pea tendrils

CHILLI DRESSING

1 tablespoon sweet chilli sauce
2 tablespoons lime juice
2 red Thai chillies, chopped finely
1/4 cup (60ml) peanut oil
1 tablespoon sugar

1 Combine chicken, soy and garlic in large bowl; cover, refrigerate 3 hours or overnight.

2 Drain chicken; discard marinade. Heat oil in large pan; cook chicken, in batches, until browned all over and cooked through. Cover chicken; rest 5 minutes, slice thinly.

3 Meanwhile, whisk eggs in medium bowl with onion. Pour half of egg mixture into heated large non-stick pan; cook, tilting pan, over medium heat until egg mixture is almost set. Turn, cook further 2 minutes. Repeat with remaining mixture.

4 Roll omelettes together; cut into thin slices.

5 Gently toss chicken and omelette in large bowl with tat soi, tendrils and three-quarters of the dressing. Serve remaining dressing separately.

chilli dressing Combine ingredients in screw-top jar; shake well.

SERVES 4

per serve 31.6g fat; 2034kJ

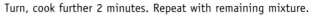

SNOW PEA TENDRILS

Tilting pan when cooking omelette

Slicing rolled omelettes

FORK FROM THE BAY TREE KITCHEN SHOP

Spooning salsa into avocado halves

prawn salad with gazpacho salsa

PREPARATION TIME 35 MINUTES • COOKING TIME 2 MINUTES

Saffron, the dried stigma from the crocus flower, is the world's costliest spice. Buy it in small amounts and keep it, sealed tightly, in the refrigerator to preserve its freshness.

1kg cooked king prawns

2 medium (500g) avocados

GAZPACHO SALSA

2 (260g) Lebanese cucumbers, seeded, chopped finely

2 medium (380g) tomatoes, seeded, chopped finely

1 clove garlic, crushed

1 tablespoon olive oil

2 tablespoons tomato juice

1 tablespoon raspberry vinegar

SAFFRON MAYONNAISE

2 tablespoons lemon juice

1/4 teaspoon saffron threads

2 egg yolks

1 tablespoon Dijon mustard

1/3 cup (80ml) olive oil

1 tablespoon finely chopped fresh dill

1 tablespoon warm water

1 Make salsa and mayonnaise, as directed below, first.

2 Shell and devein prawns, leaving tails and heads intact.

3 Halve avocados; discard seeds.

4 Divide three-quarters of the salsa among serving plates. Place avocado halves on top; fill avocado centres with remaining salsa and prawns, spoon mayonnaise over prawns.

gazpacho salsa Combine ingredients in medium bowl; mix well.

saffron mayonnaise Gently heat juice and saffron in small pan over low heat, about 2 minutes or until juice has changed colour; cool. Blend or process strained juice, egg yolks and mustard until smooth. With motor operating, gradually add oil in thin stream until combined. Stir in dill; add the water to thin mayonnaise, if desired.

SERVES 4

per serve 56.6g fat; 3163kJ

tip Saffron mayonnaise is even better if made a day ahead; keep, covered, in refrigerator.

SAFFRON THREADS

Cutting daikon into matchstick-sized pieces

Thinly slicing barbecued pork fillet

chinese barbecued pork and noodle salad

PREPARATION TIME 35 MINUTES (plus standing time) • COOKING TIME 5 MINUTES

Because you simply slice the cooked meat for this salad, buy the best-quality pork fillet available from your nearest Asian barbecued-meat takeaway shop – don't forget to buy the pickled ginger there, too.

200g daikon

800g fresh egg noodles

1/4 cup (40g) drained pickled ginger

500g Chinese barbecued pork, sliced thinly

150g snow peas, sliced thinly

1/2 cup (75g) coarsely chopped toasted cashews

CHILLI DRESSING

2 teaspoons sambal oelek

1 teaspoon fish sauce

1/3 cup (80ml) peanut oil

1/3 cup (80ml) lime juice

1 clove garlic, crushed

1 tablespoon brown sugar

1 Cut daikon into 5cm lengths; cut lengths into matchstick-sized pieces.

2 Place noodles in large heatproof bowl, cover with boiling water, stand about 2 minutes or until just tender; drain.

3 Cut ginger into narrow strips.

4 Gently toss daikon, noodles, ginger, pork, snow peas and nuts in large bowl with dressing.

chilli dressing Combine ingredients in screw-top jar; mix well.

SERVES 4

per serve 61.2g fat; 5307kJ

tip You need to buy a medium-sized daikon, the Japanese carrot-shaped large white radish, in order to have the 200g of trimmed peeled uncooked daikon required for this recipe.

DAIKON

marinated lamb salad with lemon yogurt dressing

PREPARATION TIME 20 MINUTES (plus marinating and standing time) • COOKING TIME 10 MINUTES

750g lamb backstrap
2 cloves garlic, crushed
1 tablespoon finely chopped
 fresh mint leaves
1 tablespoon finely shredded
 lemon rind
2 tablespoons lemon juice
2 medium (400g) red capsicums
2 (260g) Lebanese cucumbers,
 sliced thinly
1 medium (170g) red onion,
 sliced thinly
100g kalamata olives, seeded
100g fetta cheese, crumbled
1 baby cos lettuce

LEMON YOGURT DRESSING
200ml yogurt
1/4 cup (60ml) lemon juice
1 clove garlic, crushed
2 tablespoons water

1 Combine lamb with garlic, mint, rind and juice in large shallow dish; cover, refrigerate 3 hours or overnight.

2 Drain lamb; discard marinade. Cook lamb in heated oiled grill pan (or on grill or barbecue) until browned all over and cooked as desired. Cover lamb, rest 5 minutes; slice thinly.

LAMB BACKSTRAP

3 Cut capsicums into diamond shapes.

4 Gently toss lamb, capsicum, cucumber, onion, olives, cheese and lettuce leaves in large bowl with dressing.

lemon yogurt dressing Whisk ingredients together in small bowl.

SERVES 4

per serve 52.8g fat; 2865kJ

Cutting capsicum into diamonds

Crumbling fetta

wheat noodle, snake bean and roasted capsicum salad

PREPARATION TIME 20 MINUTES • COOKING TIME 20 MINUTES

Stir-fry noodles or hokkien mee, found fresh in the refrigerated section of most supermarkets, can be used in place of the wheat noodles. Just rinse them under hot water to separate them, then drain thoroughly before tossing in the salad.

3 medium (600g) red capsicums

250g dried wheat noodles

350g snake beans

1 medium (170g) red onion, sliced thinly

2 tablespoons white sesame seeds, toasted

1/2 cup coarsely chopped fresh coriander leaves

SESAME-SOY DRESSING

1/4 cup (60ml) lemon juice

1/3 cup (80ml) peanut oil

1 teaspoon sesame oil

2 tablespoons rice vinegar

2 tablespoons soy sauce

1 tablespoon brown sugar

1 Quarter capsicums, remove and discard seeds and membranes. Roast under grill or in very hot oven, skin-side up, until skin blisters and blackens. Cover capsicum quarters in plastic or paper; peel away skin. Cut each quarter in half lengthways; cut pieces into thick diagonal slices.

2 Meanwhile, cook noodles in large pan of boiling water, uncovered, until just tender; drain.

3 Cut beans into 4cm lengths. Boil, steam or microwave until just tender; drain.

4 Gently toss capsicum, noodles, beans, onion, seeds and coriander in large bowl with dressing.

sesame-soy dressing Combine ingredients in screw-top jar; shake well.

SERVES 4

per serve 24g fat; 2117kJ

DRIED WHEAT NOODLES

Peeling skin off the roasted capsicum

Cutting snake beans into 4cm lengths

Cutting noodle sheet into strips

Thinly slicing salmon

grilled salmon and rice noodle salad

PREPARATION TIME 25 MINUTES (plus cooling time) • COOKING TIME 10 MINUTES

For this recipe, we bought large fresh rice noodle sheets sold packaged in pairs, weighing a kilogram in total. These are available from Asian food shops; if you can't find them, use any wide fresh rice noodle – or even fresh lasagne sheets – trimmed to the appropriate size.

500g fresh rice noodle sheet

600g fresh salmon fillet

2 lemons

1/2 cup (80g) drained bottled caperberries

350g watercress, trimmed

WASABI DRESSING

1/3 cup (80ml) lemon juice

2 teaspoons wasabi

1/3 cup (80ml) peanut oil

2 teaspoons finely chopped fresh dill

1 tablespoon finely chopped fresh chives

1　Cut noodle sheet into 4cm-wide strips. Place noodles in large heatproof bowl, cover with warm water, gently separate noodles with hands. Stand noodles 1 minute; drain, pat dry with absorbent paper.

2　Cut salmon, across the grain, into thin slices. Cut each lemon into 8 wedges.

3　Cook salmon, in batches, in heated oiled grill pan (or on grill or barbecue) until cooked as desired. Cook lemon, in batches, in same pan until browned.

4　Gently toss salmon and lemon in large bowl with caperberries, watercress and dressing.

wasabi dressing　Combine ingredients in screw-top jar; shake well.

SERVES 4

per serve　29.8g fat; 2236kJ

tip　Wasabi, Japanese horseradish, is sold in powdered or paste form; make up the powder following package directions. Increase the amount of wasabi in the dressing recipe for more bite.

CAPERBERRIES

barbecued duck and pawpaw with sweet chilli dressing

PREPARATION TIME 40 MINUTES • COOKING TIME 5 MINUTES

Ready-to-eat barbecued duck can be purchased from specialty Asian barbecue takeaway shops. Barbecued chicken can be used in place of the duck.

1kg barbecued duck
4 green onions,
   chopped finely
1 small (800g) pawpaw,
   seeded, chopped coarsely
1/3 cup (50g) shelled
   pistachios, toasted
80g mizuna

PAWPAW

SWEET CHILLI DRESSING

1/4 cup (60ml) peanut oil
1/4 cup (60ml) lime juice
2 tablespoons sweet chilli sauce
1 tablespoon finely grated
   fresh ginger
1/2 teaspoon sesame oil
1 red Thai chilli, seeded,
   chopped finely

Scraping away fat from duck skin

1 Remove all meat and skin from duck; discard bones. Scrape away fat from under skin; discard fat. Cut meat and skin into thin slices.

2 Gently toss duck, onion, pawpaw, nuts and mizuna in large bowl with dressing.

sweet chilli dressing Combine ingredients in screw-top jar; shake well.

SERVES 4

per serve 50g fat; 2507kJ

tip Keep fresh chillies in your freezer. Not only will you have some on hand whenever you need them, but they're easier to slice and chop while frozen.

Thinly slicing duck meat

Seeding the pawpaw

smoked trout and potato crisp salad

PREPARATION TIME 25 MINUTES • COOKING TIME 15 MINUTES

Tiny new (or baby) potatoes, also known as chats, are just the new growth and not a particular variety of potato. We've deep-fried them twice to give the potato slices extra-special crispness.

300g tiny new potatoes

vegetable oil, for deep-frying

3 green onions

300g finely sliced smoked trout,
 chopped coarsely

2 large (500g) tomatoes,
 seeded, chopped finely

100g baby spinach leaves

LIME PEPPER DRESSING

1/2 teaspoon cracked black pepper

1 tablespoon lime juice

1 tablespoon white wine vinegar

2 tablespoons peanut oil

1 clove garlic, crushed

Slicing potatoes with a mandoline

Cutting green onions

Deep-frying potato slices a second time

1 Using mandoline or slicing blade of your food processor, cut potatoes into paper-thin slices. Rinse potato under cold water until water runs clear; drain, pat dry with absorbent paper.

2 Heat vegetable oil in wok or medium pan; deep-fry potato, in batches, until just tender but not browned. Drain on absorbent paper.

3 Slice green onions into thin strips.

4 Just before serving, reheat oil in same pan; deep-fry drained potato, in batches, until crisp and golden-brown. Drain on absorbent paper.

5 Gently toss potato, onion, trout, tomato and spinach in large bowl with dressing.

lime pepper dressing Combine ingredients in screw-top jar; shake well.

SERVES 4

per serve 12.5g fat; 1196kJ (excludes oil for deep-frying)

tip To cut paper-thin potato slices, we used a mandoline, an Italian hand-operated slicer that comes with various cutting attachments. If you make a lot of potato chips, buy one from any kitchenware shop. Potatoes can also be sliced using the appropriate disc in your food processor.

SMOKED TROUT

Gently sealing wonton wrappers

asparagus, bocconcini and smoked chicken wonton salad

PREPARATION TIME 50 MINUTES • COOKING TIME 10 MINUTES

1/3 cup (80ml) orange juice

1/4 cup (60ml) cider vinegar

2 tablespoons olive oil

2 teaspoons Dijon mustard

1 teaspoon brown sugar

2 (260g) Lebanese cucumbers, seeded, chopped finely

4 medium (300g) egg tomatoes, seeded, chopped finely

500g fresh asparagus, trimmed

12 wonton wrappers

12 quail eggs

150g smoked chicken breast, chopped finely

vegetable oil, for deep-frying

180g bocconcini cheese, chopped

80g snow pea sprouts

1 Combine juice, vinegar, olive oil, mustard and sugar in screw-top jar; shake dressing well. Gently toss half of the dressing in small bowl with cucumber and tomato, cover; refrigerate.

2 Cook asparagus, in batches, on heated oiled grill plate (or grill or barbecue) until lightly browned; drain on absorbent paper, halve spears crossways.

3 Press wonton wrappers into lightly oiled 12-hole round-base patty pan. Break 1 egg onto each wrapper; top with rounded teaspoons of chicken. Brush edges of wrappers with water; pinch corners together above filling. Press sides of each wrapper together to form wonton "pyramid" shape.

4 Heat vegetable oil in wok or medium pan; cook wontons, three at a time, about 20 seconds or until just browned. Drain on absorbent paper.

5 Gently toss asparagus in large bowl with cheese and sprouts.

6 Divide tomato mixture among serving plates; top with asparagus mixture and wontons, drizzle with remaining dressing.

SERVES 4

per serve 24.7g fat; 1726kJ
(excludes oil for deep-frying)

tip If you can't find quail eggs, substitute ordinary eggs but, because they're too large for wonton wrappers, break and beat the eggs first, using about a teaspoon of egg for each wrapper.

QUAIL EGGS

Rolling wrappers and cutting into rounds

Peeling carrot into ribbons

duck with crunchy wonton roll-ups

PREPARATION TIME 25 MINUTES • COOKING TIME 45 MINUTES

1kg duck breasts
2 tablespoons hoisin sauce
2 tablespoons plum sauce
10 wonton wrappers
vegetable oil, for deep-frying
1 large (180g) carrot
4 green onions, chopped finely
80g snow pea sprouts
**2 medium (340g) cucumbers,
  seeded, sliced thinly**

HOISIN-PLUM DRESSING

1 tablespoon hoisin sauce
1 tablespoon plum sauce
2 tablespoons rice vinegar
2 tablespoons peanut oil

1 Place duck in large baking dish; brush with combined sauces. Bake, uncovered, in moderate oven about 45 minutes or until cooked through. Remove duck from pan; drain on absorbent paper. When cool enough to handle, cut into 5mm-thick slices.

2 Meanwhile, roll each wonton wrapper into a cylinder; cut each cylinder into 5mm-wide roll-ups.

3 Heat vegetable oil in wok or medium pan; deep-fry wonton roll-ups, in batches, until crisp and golden-brown, drain on absorbent paper.

4 Using vegetable peeler, peel carrot into long thin ribbons.

5 Gently toss roll-ups, carrot, onion and sprouts in large bowl with half of the dressing. Divide roll-up mixture among serving plates; top with alternate layers of duck and cucumber, drizzle with remaining dressing.

hoisin-plum dressing Combine ingredients in screw-top jar; shake well.

SERVES 4

per serve 72.4g fat; 3888kJ (excludes oil for deep-frying)

chicken noodle salad

PREPARATION TIME 40 MINUTES • COOKING TIME 15 MINUTES

Rice stick noodles, also known as sen lek (Thai) and ho fun (Chinese) are the flat wide noodle used traditionally in that mixed noodle Thai favourite we know as Phad Thai – a dish which had a great influence on the creation of this salad.

350g chicken breast fillets

200g rice stick noodles

1 medium (200g) yellow capsicum, sliced thinly

250g cherry tomatoes, quartered

1 (130g) Lebanese cucumber, seeded, sliced thinly

1/2 small (200g) Chinese cabbage, sliced thinly

1 small (100g) red onion, sliced thinly

1/3 cup firmly packed fresh Thai basil leaves

1/3 cup firmly packed fresh mint leaves

1/3 cup firmly packed fresh coriander leaves

KAFFIR LIME DRESSING

1/2 cup (125ml) lime juice

2 teaspoons fish sauce

1/4 cup (60ml) sweet chilli sauce

1/4 cup (60ml) peanut oil

2 teaspoons sugar

6 fresh kaffir lime leaves, sliced thinly

1 Cook chicken on heated oiled grill plate (or grill or barbecue) until browned all over and cooked through. Cover chicken; rest 5 minutes, slice thinly.

2 Meanwhile, carefully add noodles to medium heatproof bowl of boiling water; soak until just tender, drain. Toss noodles, in same medium bowl, with half of the dressing; divide among serving plates.

3 Gently toss chicken in large bowl with remaining dressing and remaining ingredients. Serve over noodles.

kaffir lime dressing Combine ingredients in screw-top jar; shake well.

SERVES 6

per serve 11.3g fat; 926kJ

UNCOOKED RICE STICK NOODLES

Thinly slicing kaffir lime leaves

soft egg, pancetta, asparagus and garlic-crumb pasta salad

PREPARATION TIME 20 MINUTES • COOKING TIME 20 MINUTES

A variation on a classic Italian recipe, this salad is as delicious as it is simple to prepare.

6 eggs
500g fresh asparagus, trimmed
100g thinly sliced pancetta
25g butter
2 cloves garlic, crushed
2 cups (140g) stale breadcrumbs
200g fresh lasagne sheets
2 tablespoons finely shredded
   fresh sage leaves
1/2 cup (125ml) olive oil

1 Place eggs in medium pan, cover with cold water; bring to boil. Simmer, uncovered, 3 minutes; drain. Rinse eggs under cold water; shell then quarter.

2 Halve asparagus crossways; boil, steam or microwave until just tender, drain.

3 Heat lightly oiled large pan; cook pancetta, in batches, until crisp, drain on absorbent paper. Chop pancetta coarsely.

4 Heat butter in same pan; cook garlic and breadcrumbs, stirring, until breadcrumbs are crisp.

5 Cut pasta into 3cm-wide strips; cook in large pan of boiling water, uncovered, until pasta is just tender, drain.

6 Combine breadcrumbs and pasta in large bowl; add egg, asparagus, pancetta, sage and oil, toss gently.

SERVES 4

per serve 45.7g fat; 2806kJ

tip You can substitute any green vegetable for the asparagus. Dried lasagne can also be used – cook until just tender, drain, then cut into strips.

SAGE LEAVES

Shelling and cutting soft-boiled eggs

Cooking pancetta until well crisped

Snapping off the woody ends of asparagus spears and peeling away tough lower skin

Grilling pears

grilled asparagus, pear and prosciutto salad

PREPARATION TIME 20 MINUTES • COOKING TIME 20 MINUTES

This exquisite combination of ingredients makes a very special snack or light lunch.

500g fresh asparagus
8 slices (120g) prosciutto
2 medium (460g) corella pears
1/4 cup coarsely chopped
  fresh chives
300g curly endive, trimmed
100g firm goat cheese

TANGY CHAMPAGNE DRESSING

1/4 cup (60ml) Champagne vinegar
2 tablespoons seeded mustard
1/4 cup (60ml) light olive oil

1 Snap ends off asparagus; if necessary, peel away tough lower skin of spears. Cook asparagus, in batches, on heated oiled grill plate (or grill or barbecue) until browned all over and just tender.

2 Cut prosciutto slices in half; cook, in batches, on same grill plate until crisp. Drain on absorbent paper.

3 Halve pears, discard cores; cut each half into four wedges. Cook pear, in batches, on same grill plate until just starting to brown both sides.

4 Gently toss asparagus, prosciutto and pear in large bowl with chives, endive and dressing; sprinkle with crumbled cheese.

tangy champagne dressing Combine ingredients in screw-top jar; shake well.

SERVES 4

per serve 21.6g fat; 1491kJ

tip For a completely different finish to this salad, use a creamy blue cheese like Bavarian Blue or Castello in place of the goat cheese.

CURLY ENDIVE

Coating lamb with crushed coriander seeds

Thinly slicing lamb

lamb and lentil salad

PREPARATION TIME 20 MINUTES (plus standing time) • COOKING TIME 30 MINUTES

*You could replace the red and brown lentils used here with any kind of beans,
chickpeas or split peas – whatever you prefer – but you'll find the salad is best
if dried and pre-cooked versions (rather than canned) are used.*

1 cup (200g) red lentils
1 cup (200g) brown lentils
1 tablespoon coriander seeds
600g lamb eye of loin
1 (130g) Lebanese cucumber,
chopped coarsely
2 trimmed (150g) celery sticks,
chopped coarsely
1 small (100g) red onion,
chopped coarsely
2 medium (380g) tomatoes,
chopped coarsely
2 teaspoons sweet paprika
2 teaspoons ground cumin
2 teaspoons ground coriander
2 tablespoons peanut oil
2 tablespoons lemon juice
1 medium butter lettuce, trimmed

1 Cook lentils, separately, uncovered, in pans of boiling water until
tender; drain. Rinse under cold water; drain.

2 Meanwhile, using a mortar and pestle or spice grinder, crush coriander
seeds. Press lamb in crushed seeds to coat all over.

3 Cook lamb, uncovered, in heated oiled large pan until browned all
over and cooked as desired. Cover; rest 5 minutes, slice thinly.

4 Gently toss lentils, lamb, cucumber, celery, onion and tomato in
large bowl with combined spices, oil and juice.

5 Serve lamb and lentil mixture in
lettuce leaves.

SERVES 4

per serve 26.4g fat; 2684kJ

BUTTER LETTUCE LEAF

citrus-flavoured beef fillet with witlof

PREPARATION TIME 20 MINUTES (plus marinating time) • COOKING TIME 15 MINUTES

Witlof is known as Belgian endive in the Americas, witloof on the Continent and, mistakenly, chicory in some other places. You can use the red or white variety (or even its near-cousin, radicchio) for this recipe.

500g beef fillet
1/2 cup (135g) marmalade
1/2 cup (125ml) orange juice
2 tablespoons brown sugar
1 clove garlic, crushed
2 medium (480g) oranges
2 tablespoons peanut oil
1/2 cup (80g) blanched almonds
2 green onions, sliced thinly
1kg witlof, leaves separated
1/4 cup (60ml) orange juice, extra

1 Cut beef into thin slices; combine in large bowl with marmalade, juice, sugar and garlic. Cover; refrigerate 3 hours or overnight.

2 Drain beef over medium bowl; reserve marinade. Remove peel, pith and seeds from oranges; cut into 1cm-thick slices.

3 Heat the oil in wok or large pan; cook nuts, stirring, until just brown. Remove from wok to large bowl.

4 Add beef, in batches, to wok; stir-fry until just browned. Place in bowl with nuts.

5 Add orange slices to same wok; cook, in batches, until just browned both sides. Place in bowl with nuts and beef, add onion; toss gently to combine.

6 Add reserved marinade to wok, bring to boil; boil 1 minute.

7 Divide witlof among serving plates; top with beef salad, drizzle with combined cooled marinade and extra juice.

SERVES 4

per serve 28.9g fat; 2698kJ

tip Beef will be easier to slice if it has been wrapped tightly in plastic wrap and placed in the freezer for an hour or so.

WITLOF

Cutting beef into thin slices

Browning orange slices in wok

lemon paprika chicken with turmeric oil

PREPARATION TIME 30 MINUTES (plus marinating and refrigeration time) • COOKING TIME 25 MINUTES

There are many different varieties of flavoured pappadums available; use one with dried chilli if you want to add a bite to the crunch!

700g chicken breast fillets

2 cloves garlic, crushed

1 tablespoon finely grated lemon rind

1/2 cup (125ml) olive oil

1 teaspoon sweet paprika

1 teaspoon ground turmeric

2 medium (340g) green cucumbers

2 red Thai chillies, chopped finely

2 tablespoons white vinegar

2 teaspoons sugar

8 pappadums

vegetable oil, for deep-frying

80g baby spinach leaves

200ml yogurt

1 tablespoon coarsely chopped fresh mint leaves

2 tablespoons coarsely chopped fresh coriander leaves

1 Combine chicken, garlic, rind, olive oil, paprika and turmeric in large bowl, cover; refrigerate 3 hours or overnight.

2 Using vegetable peeler, slice cucumbers into ribbons. Combine cucumber in medium bowl with chilli, vinegar and sugar, cover; refrigerate 20 minutes.

3 Meanwhile, remove chicken from turmeric oil marinade; reserve marinade. Cook chicken, in batches, in heated oiled large pan, until browned all over and cooked through. Cover chicken; rest 5 minutes, slice thinly.

4 Bring reserved turmeric marinade to boil in small pan, boil 1 minute; cool.

5 Deep-fry pappadums, in batches, in hot vegetable oil until puffed and crisp; drain on absorbent paper.

6 Gently toss chicken, spinach and cucumber mixture in large bowl.

7 Combine yogurt, mint and coriander in small bowl.

8 Divide pappadums among serving bowls; top with chicken mixture; drizzle with yogurt mixture and turmeric oil.

SERVES 4

per serve 35.7g fat; 2199kJ (excludes oil for deep-frying)

tip Pappadums can also be puffed in the microwave oven. Place them, two at a time, on your microwave oven turntable; cook on HIGH (100%) about 30 seconds or until crisp. Cooked pappadums can be made a day ahead if, once cooled, they are kept in an airtight container.

PAPPADUMS, BEFORE (FRONT) AND AFTER DEEP-FRYING

Flaking the drained tuna

Tossing all ingredients together just before serving

lemon tuna and farfalle salad

PREPARATION TIME 25 MINUTES • COOKING TIME 10 MINUTES

As an alternative to canned tuna, finely chopped fresh tuna can be used if you marinate it in the tapenade mixture overnight, but be aware that the fish is raw.

375g farfalle

1/4 cup (60g) olive tapenade

1 teaspoon finely grated lemon rind

3/4 cup (180ml) lemon juice

1/2 cup (125ml) extra virgin olive oil

2 tablespoons white wine vinegar

1 tablespoon sugar

1 teaspoon salt

425g can tuna in oil, drained, flaked

1 large (400g) green cucumber, seeded, chopped finely

4 trimmed (300g) celery sticks, sliced thinly

4 green onions, sliced thinly

2 red Thai chillies, seeded, chopped finely

1/3 cup finely chopped fresh mint leaves

1 Cook pasta in large pan of boiling water, uncovered, until just tender; drain. Rinse under cold water; drain.

2 Stir tapenade with rind, juice, oil, vinegar, sugar and salt in small bowl; mix well to combine.

3 Gently toss pasta and tapenade mixture in large bowl with tuna, cucumber, celery, onion, chilli and mint.

SERVES 4

per serve 44.2g fat; 3562kJ

tip Tapenade, a paste of pureed olives, is available from delicatessens. Make the tapenade mixture the day before required to allow the flavours to blend.

FARFALLE

Caramelising onion

Cutting pumpkin slices

beef, pumpkin and mushroom salad with onion chutney

PREPARATION TIME 25 MINUTES • COOKING TIME 40 MINUTES (plus resting time)

You could use beef already cut into thin strips by the butcher in this recipe.

4 large (360g) egg tomatoes, quartered

8 large (400g) cultivated mushrooms, peeled

1 clove garlic, chopped finely

1 tablespoon olive oil

40g butter

2 tablespoons brown sugar

1 large (200g) brown onion, sliced thinly

1kg butternut pumpkin

750g beef rump steak

2 tablespoons balsamic vinegar

80g baby rocket leaves

1 Place tomato and mushrooms on large oven tray; sprinkle with garlic, drizzle with oil. Bake, uncovered, in moderately hot oven about 40 minutes or until tomato is browned lightly.

2 Meanwhile, heat butter and sugar in medium pan, stirring, until sugar dissolves. Add onion; cook, stirring, until onion is soft. Simmer mixture, uncovered, about 10 minutes or until onion caramelises, stirring frequently.

3 Cut narrow top end of pumpkin into eight 5mm-thick slices. Heat oiled medium non-stick pan; cook pumpkin, in batches, until browned both sides. Drain on absorbent paper.

4 Cook beef in same pan until browned all over and cooked as desired. Remove beef from pan, cover; rest 10 minutes, slice thinly.

5 Add vinegar to pan juices; simmer, uncovered, 2 minutes. Add onion mixture to pan; stir until chutney is mixed and heated through.

6 Divide pumpkin and mushrooms among serving plates; stack with beef, tomato, onion chutney and rocket.

SERVES 4

per serve 19.3g fat; 2055kJ

CULTIVATED MUSHROOMS

ceviche

PREPARATION TIME 20 MINUTES (plus refrigeration time)

*Ceviche, also known as seviche or cebiche, is an everyday fish salad eaten throughout
the islands of the Caribbean and all over Latin America. While marinating the fish in
lime juice appears to "cook" it, be aware that the fish is raw. You will need approximately
10 limes for this recipe.*

1kg redfish fillets

1¹/₂ cups (375ml) fresh lime juice

**¹/₄ cup (40g) canned jalapeño
chilli slices, drained**

¹/₄ cup (60ml) olive oil

**1 large (250g) tomato,
chopped coarsely**

**¹/₄ cup coarsely chopped
fresh coriander leaves**

**1 small (80g) white onion,
chopped finely**

1 clove garlic, crushed

1 Remove any remaining skin or bones from
fish; cut fish into 3cm pieces.

2 Combine fish and juice in non-reactive large
bowl, cover; refrigerate 4 hours or overnight.

3 Drain fish; discard juice. Return fish to bowl,
add remaining ingredients; toss gently to
combine. Cover; refrigerate 1 hour.

SERVES 4

per serve 21.5g fat; 1841kJ

tip Fish must be marinated with the lime juice in a non-reactive bowl
(one made from glazed porcelain or glass is best), to avoid the metallic
taste that can result if marinating takes place in a stainless-steel or an
aluminium bowl. Ensure all of the fish is completely covered with juice.

BOTTLED JALAPEÑO CHILLIES

Cutting the fish

Pouring lime juice over fish

spiced lamb salad with mango dressing

PREPARATION TIME 20 MINUTES (plus marinating time) • COOKING TIME 10 MINUTES

You will need about 2 small fresh mangoes (or drained, canned mango slices) for the puree in this recipe.

750g lamb eye of loin

1 tablespoon ground cumin

1 tablespoon ground coriander

2 teaspoons ground turmeric

1/2 teaspoon hot paprika

2 teaspoons garlic salt

2 lavash

1 medium (200g) red capsicum, sliced thinly

1 medium (200g) yellow capsicum, sliced thinly

1 medium (170g) red onion, sliced thinly

2 medium (500g) avocados, sliced thinly

1 butter lettuce, trimmed

2 tablespoons fresh coriander leaves

MANGO DRESSING

1 cup (250ml) mango puree

1/2 cup (125ml) lime juice

1 Place lamb in large bowl with combined spices and salt, cover; refrigerate 30 minutes.

2 Cook lamb, uncovered, in heated oiled pan until browned all over and cooked as desired. Cover, rest 5 minutes; slice thinly.

3 Meanwhile, place lavash on oiled oven tray, bake, uncovered, in moderate oven about 5 minutes or until lightly browned. Cool; break into large pieces.

BUTTER LETTUCE

4 Divide lamb, capsicums, onion, avocado, lettuce and coriander among serving plates; drizzle with dressing. Serve with lavash.

mango dressing Combine ingredients in screw-top jar; shake well.

SERVES 4

per serve 27.9g fat; 2417kJ

Coating lamb in spices and salt

Cutting asparagus spears

beef and browned vegetable salad with mustard-seed dressing

PREPARATION TIME 10 MINUTES (plus marinating and standing time) • COOKING TIME 25 MINUTES

Mustard-seed oil is a mild-tasting oil made from the first pressing of fine yellow mustard seeds.
A nut oil such as macadamia or hazelnut can be used in place of the mustard-seed oil if you prefer.

500g beef fillet
³/4 cup (180ml) dry red wine
2 cloves garlic, crushed
500g fresh asparagus, trimmed
500g Swiss brown mushrooms
120g thinly sliced pancetta
300g snow peas
1 red mignonette lettuce

MUSTARD-SEED DRESSING

¹/3 cup (80ml) red wine vinegar
2 teaspoons seeded mustard
¹/4 cup (60ml) mustard-seed oil
¹/4 cup (60ml) olive oil

SWISS BROWN MUSHROOMS

1 Cut beef crossways into four even-sized pieces; combine with wine and garlic in large bowl. Cover; refrigerate 3 hours or overnight.

2 Drain beef; discard marinade. Cook beef, in batches, on heated oiled grill plate (or grill or barbecue) until browned all over and cooked as desired. Cover beef; rest 5 minutes, slice thinly.

3 Wipe cooled grill plate clean with absorbent paper. Oil and reheat grill plate; cook asparagus, in batches, until browned and just tender. Cut asparagus into 5cm lengths.

4 Cook mushrooms, in batches, on same grill plate until brown and just tender.

5 Cook pancetta, in batches, on same grill plate until crisp; chop coarsely.

6 Halve snow peas diagonally; boil, steam or microwave until just tender. Drain; cool.

7 Gently toss beef, asparagus, mushroom, pancetta, snow peas and lettuce in large bowl with dressing.

mustard-seed dressing Combine ingredients in screw-top jar; shake well.

SERVES 4

per serve 36.3g fat; 2297kJ

tip Swiss brown mushrooms are often labelled cremini or Roman mushrooms in the vegetable section of your supermarket. You can substitute fresh shiitake or even button mushrooms in this recipe if you like.

accompaniments

While the salads in this chapter can form tasty meals with no further ado, they also serve as the perfect partners to complement a range of hot dishes. A pasta main is positively lonely without a side salad of crisp, peppery leaves; marinated, grilled meats are never better than when served with colourful, flavoursome vegetables; and who can beat cool cucumber as an antidote to fiery mains?

grilled vegetable salad

PREPARATION TIME 15 MINUTES • COOKING TIME 20 MINUTES

2 medium (400g) green capsicums
2 medium (400g) red capsicums
2 medium (400g) yellow capsicums
1 large (300g) red onion
2 medium (240g) green zucchini
2 medium (240g) yellow zucchini
6 baby (360g) eggplants

BALSAMIC DRESSING

2 tablespoons lemon juice
1 clove garlic, crushed
1/4 cup (60ml) olive oil
2 tablespoons balsamic vinegar
1 tablespoon chopped fresh oregano leaves

1 Quarter capsicums, remove and discard seeds and membranes. Cut into thick strips. Cut onion into 8 wedges.

2 Slice zucchini and eggplants lengthways into thin slices.

3 Cook vegetables, in batches, in heated oiled grill pan (or on grill or barbecue) until browned all over and tender. Combine all vegetables in large bowl; drizzle with balsamic dressing, mix well.

balsamic dressing Combine all ingredients in screw-top jar; shake well.

SERVES 6

per serve 10.2g fat; 637kJ

serving suggestion This colourful salad goes well with the classic Italian dish osso buco – slow-cooked veal shins in a herbed vegetable sauce.

tip Make this salad the day before you intend to serve it, to infuse the grilled vegetables with the flavour of the dressing.

Slicing zucchini lengthways

Slicing baby eggplant lengthways

GREEN, YELLOW AND RED CAPSICUMS

Slicing bocconcini

Chopping capers

bocconcini and basil salad

PREPARATION TIME 15 MINUTES • COOKING TIME 2 HOURS

8 medium (600g)
   egg tomatoes, halved
1 tablespoon olive oil
1 tablespoon balsamic vinegar
1/4 teaspoon cracked
   black pepper
240g bocconcini cheese, sliced
1/4 cup loosely packed
   fresh basil leaves

CAPER DRESSING

1 tablespoon capers, drained
2 tablespoons olive oil
2 tablespoons balsamic vinegar
1 clove garlic, crushed

1 Place tomato, cut-side up, on oven tray; drizzle with oil and vinegar, sprinkle with pepper. Bake tomato, uncovered, in slow oven about 2 hours or until soft.

2 Alternate layers of tomato, cheese and basil onto serving plate; drizzle with caper dressing.

caper dressing Chop capers finely; combine capers with remaining ingredients in screw-top jar; shake well.

SERVES 4

per serve 28.4g fat; 1478kJ

serving suggestion A great accompaniment to traditional pasta dishes such as spinach and ricotta ravioli.

BOCCONCINI

baby rocket and parmesan salad

PREPARATION TIME 25 MINUTES • COOKING TIME 3 MINUTES

This salad is found on the menus of Italian restaurants everywhere in the world. The combination of the rocket's appealing bitterness and the sweet acidity of the balsamic vinegar offer a welcome foil to the richness of many Italian main courses.

60g parmesan cheese

200g baby rocket leaves

80g semi-dried tomatoes, halved lengthways

1/4 cup (40g) pine nuts, toasted

1/4 cup (60ml) balsamic vinegar

1/4 cup (60ml) extra virgin olive oil

1 Using vegetable peeler, shave cheese into wide, long pieces.

2 Combine rocket with tomato and nuts in large bowl; add cheese, drizzle with combined vinegar and oil, toss gently.

SERVES 8

per serve 16g fat; 744kJ

tips Baby spinach leaves can be substituted for rocket.

• To keep rocket crisp, rinse under cold water. Place in an airtight plastic bag and refrigerate for several hours or overnight.

• Nuts of any kind can easily be toasted on top of the stove by stirring them in a dry heavy-base pan over medium-to-high heat briefly, until they are just golden-brown.

SEMI-DRIED TOMATOES

Shaving parmesan cheese

Toasting pine nuts

shredded, grated great slaws

A new take on an old favourite can make a welcome change at mealtimes. So three delicious versions of coleslaw, with a range of ingredients that lend an international flavour, will have you tucking into your meal with renewed gusto.

pamela's coleslaw

PREPARATION TIME 20 MINUTES

This is a perfect coleslaw for people who don't care for creamy salad dressings.

1 medium (1.5kg) white cabbage, shredded finely
15 green onions, chopped finely
2 red Thai chillies, seeded, chopped finely
1 cup coarsely chopped fresh mint leaves
1/2 cup coarsely chopped fresh flat-leaf parsley
1/4 cup coarsely chopped fresh coriander leaves

LEMON DRESSING

1/4 cup (60ml) lemon juice
1 tablespoon Dijon mustard
1/2 cup (125ml) peanut oil

1 Combine cabbage in large bowl with onion, chilli and herbs.

2 Pour lemon dressing over salad; toss to combine.

lemon dressing Combine all ingredients in screw-top jar; shake well.

SERVES 8

per serve 15.2g fat; 747kJ

serving suggestion Great for large gatherings, this coleslaw goes well with barbecued steak or lamb chops.

tip Use rubber gloves when seeding and chopping chillies, as they can burn your skin.

red cabbage, apple and caraway coleslaw

PREPARATION TIME 15 MINUTES

This salad, of German origin, can be served either warm or cold.

2 medium (300g) green apples
1/2 medium (800g) red cabbage, shredded finely
2 tablespoons caraway seeds, toasted
2 teaspoons Dijon mustard
1/2 cup (125ml) olive oil
2 tablespoons raspberry vinegar

1 Core unpeeled apples; cut into matchstick-size pieces.

2 Combine apple in large bowl with cabbage and seeds; drizzle with combined remaining ingredients, toss to combine.

SERVES 8

per serve 15.6g fat; 738kJ

serving suggestion Perfect with a roast loin of pork.

tip If your supermarket doesn't stock raspberry vinegar, use any fruit-flavoured vinegar in this recipe.

crunchy fried noodle coleslaw

PREPARATION TIME 35 MINUTES

Picnicking? Carry the noodles and jar of dressing separately to the rest of this salad, then toss them all together when you're ready to eat.

10 trimmed (150g) radishes

1 large (350g) red capsicum, sliced thinly

1 small (450g) Chinese cabbage, shredded

6 green onions, chopped finely

1 cup (80g) bean sprouts

¹/₂ cup (70g) slivered almonds, toasted

2 x 100g packets fried noodles

SWEET-SOUR DRESSING

²/₃ cup (160ml) peanut oil

2 tablespoons white vinegar

2 tablespoons brown sugar

2 tablespoons soy sauce

2 teaspoons sesame oil

1 clove garlic, crushed

1 Slice radishes into matchstick-size pieces.

2 Combine radish in large bowl with capsicum, cabbage, onion, sprouts, nuts and noodles.

3 Pour sweet-sour dressing over salad; toss to combine.

sweet-sour dressing Combine all ingredients in screw-top jar; shake well.

SERVES 8

per serve 37.1g fat; 1914kJ

serving suggestion Serve indoors with stir-fried beef or outdoors with barbecued hot dogs.

tip For extra heat, try adding 1 tablespoon Thai sweet chilli sauce or 1 finely chopped chilli to the dressing.

red cabbage, apple and caraway coleslaw (far left)
pamela's coleslaw (above left)
crunchy fried noodle coleslaw (above)

japanese cucumber salad

PREPARATION TIME 25 MINUTES (plus standing time) • COOKING TIME 10 MINUTES

Wakame is one of many dried seaweeds used by the Japanese in cooking. Green-black in colour and extremely rich in calcium, wakame can be eaten, as here, shredded on top of salads or reconstituted in hot water and eaten as a vegetable. It is available from Japanese and some other Asian food shops; you can use any edible dried seaweed or kelp in its place.

2 large (800g) green cucumbers

1 tablespoon coarse cooking salt

¹/₃ cup (80ml) mirin

¹/₄ cup (60ml) rice vinegar

1 tablespoon soy sauce

1 tablespoon dashi

2 teaspoons sugar

200g firm tofu

vegetable oil, for deep-frying

2 teaspoons shredded wakame

1 Cut cucumbers in half lengthways; remove seeds, cut into thin slices. Combine cucumber and salt in bowl; cover, refrigerate 30 minutes.

2 Meanwhile, combine mirin, vinegar, soy, dashi and sugar in small pan. Stir over low heat, without boiling, about 5 minutes or until sugar dissolves; cool.

3 Cut tofu into 3cm cubes. Heat oil in medium pan; deep-fry tofu, in batches, until browned. Drain on absorbent paper.

4 Rinse cucumber under cold water; drain.

5 Just before serving, combine cucumber, wakame and mirin mixture in medium bowl; toss gently to combine. Divide tofu among serving plates; top with cucumber salad.

SERVES 4

per serve 5.9g fat; 547kJ (excludes oil for deep-frying)

serving suggestion Serve with a platter of mixed sashimi (include salmon, tuna and a firm white fish), soy sauce, wasabi paste and pink pickled ginger.

tip The cucumber can be combined with salt for up to 3 hours; the longer the mixture stands, the more soft and delicate the cucumber becomes.

WAKAME (DRIED SEAWEED)

Salting sliced cucumber

Shredding wakame

Cooking cumin and seeds

Peeling ginger

lentil and split pea salad

PREPARATION TIME 10 MINUTES (plus soaking time) • COOKING TIME 40 MINUTES

Here's a salad variation on the classic Indian dish of spicy mixed dhal.

1/2 cup (100g) yellow split peas

1/2 cup (100g) green split peas

1/2 cup (100g) red lentils

1/4 cup (60ml) peanut oil

1 teaspoon ground cumin

1 teaspoon coriander seeds

2 teaspoons black mustard seeds

2 cloves garlic, crushed

1 teaspoon grated fresh ginger

1 medium (170g) red onion, finely chopped

1/4 cup (60ml) lime juice

1/3 cup finely chopped fresh mint leaves

1 Cover yellow and green peas with cold water in large bowl; soak overnight.

2 Rinse peas under cold water then cook in medium pan of boiling water, uncovered, until tender. Drain, cool.

3 Meanwhile, rinse lentils under cold water then cook in small pan of boiling water, uncovered, until tender. Drain, cool.

4 Heat 1 tablespoon of the oil in small pan; cook cumin and seeds, stirring, until they start to pop. Add garlic and ginger; cook, stirring, until fragrant.

5 Combine lentils, peas and spices in large bowl; add remaining oil, onion, juice and mint, toss gently to combine.

SERVES 6

per serve 10.8g fat; 1013kJ

serving suggestion Serve with pappadums and barbecued spareribs or chicken wings.

tip Cook the peas and lentils early in the day then place them together in a single bowl; cover and refrigerate until you're ready to finish the recipe.

RED LENTILS, GREEN SPLIT PEAS, YELLOW SPLIT PEAS (FRONT TO BACK)

Cubing potatoes

Chopping tarragon

potato salad

PREPARATION TIME 25 MINUTES (plus cooling time) • COOKING TIME 20 MINUTES

7 large (2kg) pontiac potatoes

**1 large (200g) brown onion,
chopped finely**

6 green onions, chopped finely

**2 tablespoons finely chopped
fresh tarragon leaves**

**5 hard-boiled eggs,
chopped coarsely**

3/4 cup (180ml) mayonnaise

3/4 cup (180ml) sour cream

1 tablespoon seeded mustard

1 clove garlic, crushed

**2 tablespoons finely
chopped fresh chives**

1 Peel potatoes; chop into 2cm cubes. Boil, steam or microwave potato until just tender, drain; cool.

2 Place potato in large bowl with onions, tarragon, egg and combined remaining ingredients; toss gently to combine.

SERVES 8

per serve 23g fat; 1555kJ

serving suggestion This creamy potato salad is delicious with grilled sausages and caramelised onions. Try some of the new gourmet sausages such as rosemary and lamb, or fennel and pork.

tip Keep potatoes submerged in cold water after peeling, to avoid discolouration.

PONTIAC POTATOES

celeriac and apple salad

PREPARATION TIME 35 MINUTES

*Celeriac is a wonderfully earthy winter root vegetable that is also delicious
mashed, like potatoes, with plenty of cream and butter, and a dash of nutmeg.*

2 egg yolks

1 clove garlic, crushed

1/2 teaspoon salt

**1 teaspoon finely grated
    lemon rind**

2 tablespoons lemon juice

1 cup (250ml) extra virgin olive oil

1 teaspoon bottled horseradish

500g celeriac, trimmed, peeled

1 large (200g) red apple

**2 medium (240g) carrots,
    grated coarsely**

**1 cup (100g) walnuts, toasted,
    chopped roughly**

1/4 cup chopped fresh parsley

**1 bunch (15g) fresh chives,
    cut into 7cm lengths**

1 Blend or process yolks, garlic, salt, rind and juice until combined. With motor operating, gradually add oil; process until dressing thickens and is smooth. Stir in horseradish.

2 Using a mandoline or sharp knife, cut celeriac and apple into very thin slices; cut slices into matchstick-size pieces. Place in large bowl of water to prevent discolouration.

3 Place drained celeriac and apple in large bowl with carrot, nuts, parsley, chives and horseradish dressing; toss gently to combine.

SERVES 4

per serve 80g fat; 3351kJ

tip It's worth investing in a mandoline if you're a serious cook. This hand-operated machine has adjustable razor-sharp blades for precise cutting, julienning and slicing, and is available from kitchenware shops.

CELERIAC

Slicing celeriac on a mandoline

Cutting apple into matchstick-size pieces

tempting rice salads

Versatile rice proves how easily a deliciously different salad can be prepared in a hurry – just add your choice of ingredients to render a rice salad creamy and luscious or crunchy and supremely healthy.

brown rice salad

PREPARATION TIME 15 MINUTES
• COOKING TIME 15 MINUTES

You will need to cook approximately 2/3 cup brown rice for this recipe.

500g small cooked prawns

2 cups (200g) cooked brown rice

1 medium (200g) red capsicum, chopped finely

3 green onions, sliced finely

2 trimmed (150g) celery sticks, chopped finely

2 tablespoons lemon juice

2 tablespoons light olive oil

2 tablespoons cream

2 tablespoons finely chopped fresh chives

1 teaspoon sugar

1 Shell and devein prawns; chop.

2 Place prawns in large bowl with rice, capsicum, onion, celery and combined remaining ingredients; toss gently to combine.

SERVES 8

per serve 7.5g fat; 603kJ

white rice salad

PREPARATION TIME 15 MINUTES
• COOKING TIME 5 MINUTES

You will need to cook approximately 1 cup white long-grain rice for this recipe.

1 (400g) corn cob

3 cups (300g) cooked white
   long-grain rice

1 medium (200g) red capsicum,
   chopped finely

1 medium (200g) yellow
   capsicum, chopped finely

1 medium (200g) green capsicum,
   chopped finely

2 medium (380g) tomatoes,
   seeded, chopped finely

4 (60g) radishes,
   chopped finely

1 small (100g) red onion,
   chopped finely

1 medium (250g) avocado,
   chopped finely

1/3 cup (80ml) lime juice

2 tablespoons peanut oil

1/4 cup finely chopped fresh
   coriander leaves

1 Remove husk and silk from
   corn; boil, steam or microwave
   until just tender, cut kernels
   from cob.

2 Place corn in large bowl with
   remaining ingredients; toss
   gently to combine.

SERVES 8

per serve 11g fat; 990kJ

wild rice salad

PREPARATION TIME 15 MINUTES • COOKING TIME 25 MINUTES

Wild rice, with its distinctive, long, black grains, was for centuries a staple food for various American Indian nations. These days, it is commercially grown around the world (including Australia) and can be found in most supermarkets.

1 cup (180g) uncooked wild rice

20g butter

250g button mushrooms, sliced

1 clove garlic, crushed

2 tablespoons dry red wine

3 trimmed (225g) celery sticks

1 cup (100g) pecans,
   halved lengthways

1/2 cup (85g) raisins

2 tablespoons red wine vinegar

1 teaspoon grated orange rind

1/4 cup (60ml) orange juice

1/4 cup light olive oil

1 teaspoon sugar

1 Cook rice in boiling water about
   20 minutes or until tender, drain.

2 Heat butter in large pan; cook
   mushrooms and garlic, stirring,
   until browned. Add wine; cook,
   stirring, about 1 minute or until
   wine has almost evaporated

3 Cut celery into thin slices; place
   in large bowl with rice, mushroom
   mixture, nuts, raisins and
   combined remaining ingredients;
   toss gently to combine.

SERVES 8

per serve 12.4g fat; 1040kJ

serving suggestion This salad is
a wonderful addition to a picnic.

brown rice salad (*above left*)
wild rice salad (*below left*)
white rice salad (*above*)

pasta salad

PREPARATION TIME 30 MINUTES • COOKING TIME 15 MINUTES

We used shell-shaped pasta for this salad but you can use any small pasta you like – whether it's tubular, like elbow macaroni, or a solid shape, like bow-ties or spirals.

SHELL PASTA

375g shell pasta

6 bacon rashers

1¹/₂ cups (375ml) mayonnaise

¹/₃ cup (90g) seeded mustard

³/₄ cup (180ml) buttermilk

3 trimmed (225g) celery sticks, sliced thinly

1 large (350g) red capsicum, chopped finely

1 bunch (15g) fresh chives, chopped finely

2 tablespoons finely chopped fresh flat-leaf parsley

1 Cook pasta in large pan of boiling water, uncovered, until just tender. Cool.

2 Meanwhile, remove and discard rind from bacon then cut into small pieces. Cook bacon, stirring, in heated medium pan until brown and crisp; drain on absorbent paper.

3 Whisk mayonnaise, mustard and buttermilk in large bowl.

4 Add pasta, bacon and remaining ingredients to bowl; toss gently to combine.

SERVES 6

per serve 19.5g fat; 1736kJ

serving suggestion A big bowl of this salad is a splendid accompaniment to grilled or barbecued chicken.

tips Rinse cooked, drained pasta under warm water, then under cold water, to prepare salad more quickly.

• Blend about 2 teaspoons of your favourite curry powder with the mayonnaise mixture for another flavour variation.

Removing rind and chopping bacon

Blending mustard, mayonnaise and buttermilk

mesclun salad

PREPARATION TIME 10 MINUTES

This new take on the old "quarter-of-an-iceberg" theme is a green salad made with mesclun. Sometimes called mixed small salad leaves in shops, it is just that: a mixture of various lettuces, other greens such as baby beetroot leaves or baby spinach leaves, and a sprinkling of edible flowers such as nasturtiums or marigolds.

250g mesclun

VINAIGRETTE

¹/₂ cup (125ml) olive oil

**¹/₂ cup (125ml) white
    wine vinegar**

**¹/₄ cup finely chopped fresh
    flat-leaf parsley**

2 teaspoons Dijon mustard

1 Gently rinse mesclun in cold water; dry thoroughly in salad spinner.

2 Place mesclun in large serving bowl; add vinaigrette, toss gently.

vinaigrette Combine all ingredients in a screw-top jar or bottle with a tight-fitting stopper; shake well.

SERVES 8

per serve 14.9g fat; 567kJ

serving suggestion Grilled mixed mushrooms turn this simple salad into a main meal. Alternatively, just stack the salad with slices of poached chicken breast and smoked mozzarella, and scatter hazelnuts over top.

MESCLUN

Spinning salad leaves

Shaking vinaigrette

Slicing egg tomatoes finely

Sprinkling salt over salad

sliced tomato, basil and red onion salad

PREPARATION TIME 15 MINUTES

This salad is best when assembled and kept, covered, in the refrigerator up to 3 hours before serving time so that the delightful piquancy of the flavours can blend.

4 large (360g) egg tomatoes, sliced finely

1 small (100g) red onion, sliced finely

2 tablespoons small fresh basil leaves

pinch salt

pinch cracked black pepper

pinch sugar

2 teaspoons balsamic vinegar

2 teaspoons extra virgin olive oil

1 Alternate layers of tomato, onion and basil on serving plate; sprinkle with salt, pepper and sugar. Drizzle with vinegar and oil.

SERVES 4

per serve 2g fat; 153kJ

serving suggestion This refreshing salad makes a great summer lunch when served with grilled chicken. It also goes well with a big bowl of spaghetti simply dressed with fresh herbs and oil.

SMALL BASIL LEAVES

brilliant bean salads

Beyond the 4-bean mix: these fabulous bean salads quicken the pulse and shed new light on an old staple – you'll wonder how you ever lived without them.

jamaican black bean salad

PREPARATION TIME 20 MINUTES (plus soaking and cooling time) • COOKING TIME 45 MINUTES

Dried black beans are also called turtle beans; these full-flavoured dried beans bear no resemblance to the fermented soy beans, also known as black beans, that are commonly used in Chinese cooking.

2 cups (400g) dried black beans

5 medium (375g) egg tomatoes, seeded, chopped finely

250g yellow teardrop tomatoes, chopped

75g baby spinach leaves, shredded

1 medium (170g) red onion, chopped finely

4 green onions, chopped finely

CHILLI DRESSING

1 clove garlic, quartered

1/3 cup (80ml) lime juice

1/2 teaspoon sugar

2 tablespoons white vinegar

1/3 cup (80ml) olive oil

2 tablespoons finely chopped fresh coriander leaves

1/2 teaspoon cayenne pepper

1 Cover beans with cold water in large bowl; soak overnight, drain.

2 Cook beans in large pan of boiling water, uncovered, about 45 minutes or until tender; drain, cool.

3 Place beans in large bowl with tomatoes, spinach and onions; add chilli dressing, toss gently to combine.

chilli dressing Blend or process garlic, juice, sugar, vinegar and oil until dressing thickens slightly; stir in coriander and pepper.

SERVES 8

per serve 10.6g fat; 981kJ

serving suggestion This salad also makes a wonderful salsa served with char-grilled pork and warm flour tortillas.

roasted tomato and cannellini bean salad

PREPARATION TIME 15 MINUTES (plus soaking time) • COOKING TIME 45 MINUTES

We used dried cannellini beans but you can substitute four 300g cans of any type of white beans, drained and rinsed, in this recipe.

2 cups (400g) dried cannellini beans

6 large (540g) egg tomatoes, quartered

1/3 cup (80ml) olive oil

1/2 teaspoon cracked black pepper

1 tablespoon finely grated lemon rind

1/4 cup whole fresh basil leaves

13/4 cups (210g) black seeded olives, halved

1 clove garlic, crushed

1/3 cup (80ml) lemon juice

1 teaspoon sugar

1 Cover beans with cold water in large bowl; soak overnight, drain.

2 Cook beans in large pan of boiling water, uncovered, about 45 minutes or until tender; drain, cool.

3 Meanwhile, place tomato in large baking dish; drizzle with half of the oil, sprinkle with pepper. Bake, uncovered, in very hot oven about 30 minutes or until soft.

4 Place beans and tomato in large bowl with rind, basil, olives and remaining ingredients; toss gently to combine.

SERVES 8

per serve 12g fat; 1048kJ

serving suggestion Cannellini bean salad complements grilled seafood or poultry.

jamaican black bean salad *(top)*
roasted tomato and cannellini bean salad *(centre)*
greek dried bean salad *(bottom)*

greek dried bean salad

PREPARATION TIME 15 MINUTES
(plus soaking and cooling time)
• COOKING TIME 45 MINUTES

Called "mavromatiki salata" in its country of origin, this delightful black-eye bean salad is often served as part of a mezze, that scrumptious collection of dips, salads and tidbits eaten as a first course or as a meal on their own.

2 cups (400g) black-eye beans

1 large (350g) yellow capsicum

8 medium (600g) egg tomatoes, seeded, chopped coarsely

2 medium (340g) red onions, chopped finely

1¹/₂ cups (240g) kalamata olives, seeded, sliced thinly

³/₄ cup coarsely chopped fresh flat-leaf parsley

¹/₂ cup (125ml) red wine vinegar

2 cloves garlic, crushed

1 cup (250ml) extra virgin olive oil

1 Cover beans with cold water in large bowl; soak overnight, drain.

2 Cook beans in large pan of boiling water, uncovered, about 45 minutes or until tender; drain, cool.

3 Meanwhile, quarter capsicum, remove and discard seeds and membranes. Roast under grill or in very hot oven, skin-side up, until skin blisters and blackens. Cover capsicum pieces in plastic or paper for 5 minutes, peel away skin, cut into thick strips.

4 Place beans in large bowl with capsicum and remaining ingredients; toss gently to combine.

SERVES 8

per serve 31.7g fat; 1407kJ

serving suggestion Serve this as part of a mezze, just like they do in Greece.

tip Black-eye beans (sometimes called black-eye peas) are small, beige-coloured beans having a black "dot" in the curve of their kidney-shape; they have a similar flavour to cannellini beans, and one can be substituted for the other.

Trimming outer leaves

Removing hairy choke

crisp-fried artichokes with lemon

PREPARATION TIME 15 MINUTES • COOKING TIME 15 MINUTES

4 medium (800g) globe artichokes
1/4 cup (60ml) lemon juice
vegetable oil, for deep-frying
1 clove garlic, crushed

GLOBE ARTICHOKES

1 Trim base of each artichoke, leaving about 2cm of stem. Remove tough outer leaves, trim tips of remaining leaves. Pull away some inside leaves, then scoop out hairy choke from centre with spoon.

2 Brush artichokes with 1 tablespoon of the juice. Place artichokes, cut-side down, on board, spreading leaves outward; gently press down to flatten.

3 Heat oil in large pan over medium heat; deep-fry artichokes, cut-side down, 5 minutes. Turn artichokes; cook about 5 minutes or until tender; remove from pan.

4 Reheat oil over high heat; when very hot, return artichokes to pan, deep-fry about 5 minutes or until crisp and golden brown. Drain on absorbent paper.

5 Place artichokes on serving plate; drizzle with combined remaining juice and garlic. Serve hot.

SERVES 4

per serve 0.2g fat; 85kJ (excludes oil for deep-frying)

serving suggestion Char-grilled beef or lamb kebabs are perfect with these artichokes, or they can be served as part of an antipasto platter.

tip Tender baby artichokes are the best choice for this recipe. If the artichokes you buy come with a long section of stem still attached, don't discard it before you try peeling and deep-frying it – cut it into wheels. Absolutely delicious!

moroccan-style green tomato and couscous salad

PREPARATION TIME 15 MINUTES (plus standing time) • COOKING TIME 15 MINUTES

You can substitute almonds for the pistachios, if desired.

2 medium (380g) green tomatoes
1 tablespoon olive oil
60g butter
2 teaspoons ground cumin
2 teaspoons ground coriander
1¹/₂ cups (300g) couscous
1 cup (250ml) boiling water
¹/₃ cup (50g) pine nuts, toasted
¹/₃ cup (50g) shelled pistachios,
**   toasted, chopped coarsely**
1 small (100g) red onion,
**   chopped finely**
¹/₃ cup loosely packed fresh
**   coriander leaves**

1 Cut tomatoes into 8 wedges. Heat the oil in large pan; cook tomato, stirring, about 5 minutes or until browned lightly. Add butter; cook, stirring, until butter is melted. Stir in combined spices; cook, stirring, until fragrant. Remove tomato; reserve butter mixture.

2 Combine couscous, reserved butter mixture and the boiling water in medium heatproof bowl, stand 5 minutes; fluff couscous with fork to separate grains.

3 Just before serving, place all ingredients in large bowl; toss gently to combine.

SERVES 4

per serve 33.7g fat; 2433kJ
serving suggestion Serve this delicious salad with grilled lamb cutlets and wedges of toasted pide.

GREEN TOMATOES

Fluffing couscous

Shelling and chopping pistachios

french bean salad

PREPARATION TIME 10 MINUTES • COOKING TIME 8 MINUTES

*The beauty of this recipe is that, although making it is simplicity itself,
the look and taste are that of the finest French cuisine.*

800g green beans

**1 medium (170g) red onion,
chopped finely**

1 clove garlic, crushed

1 tablespoon Dijon mustard

2 tablespoons lemon juice

1/3 cup (80ml) olive oil

**2 tablespoons coarsely chopped
fresh flat-leaf parsley**

1 Top and tail beans. Boil, steam or microwave until just tender; drain. Rinse
beans in cold water immediately; drain. Combine with onion in large bowl.

2 Meanwhile, whisk remaining ingredients together in small bowl;
pour over bean mixture, toss gently to combine.

SERVES 4

per serve 19.6g fat; 951kJ

serving suggestion Serve with char-grilled pork chops and creamy
mashed kumara.

tip For a more colourful salad, combine 400g green beans and
400g butter beans.

Topping and tailing beans

Finely chopping red onion

Whisking vinaigrette

Removing hazelnut skins

Sieving raspberry vinaigrette

watermelon and hazelnut salad with raspberry vinaigrette

PREPARATION TIME 25 MINUTES

¹/₃ cup (50g) unroasted hazelnuts

¹/₂ medium (1kg) seedless watermelon

150g butter lettuce, torn

300g lamb's lettuce, torn

150g fresh raspberries

RASPBERRY VINAIGRETTE

150g raspberries

²/₃ cup (160ml) hazelnut oil

¹/₄ cup (60ml) raspberry vinegar

1 Roast nuts on ungreased oven tray, uncovered, in moderate oven about 7 minutes or until lightly toasted. Wrap nuts in tea towel; rub off skins, chop nuts coarsely.

2 Cut watermelon into 2cm chunks.

3 Combine watermelon in large bowl with lettuces and raspberries; drizzle with raspberry vinaigrette, sprinkle with nuts.

raspberry vinaigrette Blend or process all ingredients until pureed; push vinaigrette through sieve into small bowl.

SERVES 4

per serve 38.7g fat; 1754kJ

serving suggestion This fresh salad is a perfect complement to rich meat dishes.

tip Lamb's lettuce is also known as lamb's tongue, corn salad or mache; it has a distinctive nutty taste and its leaves are delicate and tender.

LAMB'S LETTUCE

glossary

Bacon rashers also known as bacon slices; made from pork side, cured and smoked. Streaky bacon is the fatty end of a bacon rasher (slice), without the lean (eye) meat.

Beans

BLACK also known as turtle beans or black kidney beans, they are an earthy-flavoured dried bean different from the better-known Chinese black beans (which are fermented soy beans). Most used in Mexico, South- and Central-America and the Caribbean, especially in soups and stews.

BUTTER also called wax or yellow beans, they are a variety of green or French bean, cooked and eaten in similar ways.

CANNELLINI (BUTTER) small, dried white bean similar to other *Phaseolus vulgaris* (great northern, navy and haricot beans).

KIDNEY have a floury texture and sweet flavour; colour can vary from pink to maroon.

REFRIED pinto beans cooked twice: soaked and boiled then mashed and fried, traditionally in lard. A Mexican staple, "frijoles refritos" or refried beans are available canned in supermarkets. Mexe-Beans is the trade name for a canned pinto bean in chilli sauce mixture.

SNAKE about 40cm long, thin, round green beans, Asian in origin; having a taste similar to string beans and runner beans.

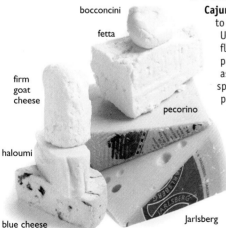

bocconcini

fetta

firm goat cheese

pecorino

haloumi

blue cheese

Jarlsberg

Bean sprouts also known as bean shoots; new growths of assorted beans and seeds germinated for consumption as sprouts. Readily available are mung bean, soy bean, alfalfa and snow pea sprouts.

Beef, minced also known as ground beef.

Bok choy also called pak choi or Chinese chard; has a mild mustard taste and is good braised or in stir-fries. Baby bok choy is also available.

Breadcrumbs

PACKAGED fine-textured, crunchy, purchased, white breadcrumbs.

STALE one- or two-day-old bread made into crumbs by grating, blending or processing.

Burghul also known as bulghur wheat; hulled steamed wheat kernels that, once dried, are crushed into various size grains. Used in Middle-Eastern dishes such as kibbeh and tabbouleh.

Butter use salted or unsalted ("sweet") butter; 125g is equal to 1 stick butter.

Cajun seasoning used to give an authentic USA-Deep-South spicy flavour to food, this packaged blend of assorted herbs and spices can include paprika, basil, onion, fennel, thyme, cayenne and tarragon.

Calamari squid.

Caperberries fruit formed after caper buds have flowered; sold pickled.

bottled sliced jalapeños

caperberries

pickled ginger

capers

kalamata olives

pickled green chillies

niçoise olives

pickled daikon

Capers the grey-green buds of a warm-climate (usually Mediterranean) shrub, used to enhance dressings and sauces with their piquancy. Sold either dried and salted or pickled in a vinegar brine. If salted, rinse and drain before use; if pickled, drain before use.

Capsicum also known as bell pepper or pepper. Membranes and seeds should be discarded.

Cardamom native to India and used extensively in its cuisine; can be purchased in pod, seed or ground form. Has a distinctive, aromatic, sweetly rich flavour and is one of the world's most expensive spices.

Celeriac tuberous root with brown skin, white flesh and a celery-like flavour.

Cheese

BLUE VEIN mould-treated cheese mottled with blue veining; many varieties, ranging from firm, crumbly and strong-flavoured to mild, creamy and brie-like.

BOCCONCINI small rounds of fresh "baby" mozzarella; a delicate, semi-soft, white cheese traditionally made in Italy from buffalo milk. Spoils rapidly so must be kept under refrigeration, in brine, for one or two days at most.

FETTA Greek in origin; a crumbly-textured goat or sheep milk cheese with a sharp, salty taste.

GOAT made from goat milk; has an earthy, strong taste and is available in both soft and firm textures.

HALOUMI firm, cream-coloured sheep milk cheese matured in brine; somewhat like a minty, salty fetta, haloumi can be grilled or fried, briefly, without breaking down.

JARLSBERG Norwegian cheese made from cow milk; firm, with large holes and a mild, nutty taste.

PARMESAN sharp-tasting, dry, hard cheese, made from skim or part-skim milk and aged for at least a year. Parmigiano Reggiano, from Italy, aged a minimum three years, is one of the best.

PECORINO hard, dry, sharp-tasting yellow cheese. Made originally from sheep milk, it is now made with cow milk. If unavailable, use parmesan.

SOFT BLUE VEIN sweet rather than acidic, double-cream blue cheese; Blue Castello is an example.

Chickpeas also called garbanzos, hummus or channa; an irregularly round, sandy-coloured legume used extensively in Mediterranean and Latin cooking.

Chillies available in many types and sizes. Use rubber gloves when seeding and chopping fresh chillies as they can burn your skin. Removing seeds and membranes lessens the heat level.

JALAPEÑO fairly hot green chilli, available in brine or fresh from specialty greengrocers.

PICKLED GREEN served in Lebanese mezzes and Italian appetisers; is sweet and hot.

THAI sometimes called "scuds" because of their fire power! Small and green or red in colour, they are available fresh in supermarkets. Great in South-East Asian cooking.

Chinese barbecued pork also known as char siew. This pork has a sweet-sticky coating made from soy sauce, sherry, five-spice and hoisin sauce. It is available from Asian food stores.

Chives related to the onion and leek, with subtle onion flavour. Chives and flowering chives are interchangeable.

GARLIC have flat leaves and a stronger flavour than chives.

Ciabatta dense, crusty loaf of Italian origin, baked in a wood-fired oven; also baked as small rolls.

Coconut
CREAM available in cans and cartons; made from coconut flesh and water. Thicker and richer than coconut milk. Use within 24 hours of opening.

MILK unsweetened coconut milk available in cans.

Corella pear miniature dessert pear up to 10cm long.

Corn chips packaged snack food that evolved from fried corn tortilla pieces.

Corn Flake Crumbs packaged product of crushed corn flakes, used to coat chicken, etc.

Cornmeal ground dried corn (maize); similar to polenta but slightly coarser. One can be substituted for the other, but textures will vary.

Couscous fine, grain-like cereal, originally from North Africa; made from semolina.

Cream
FRESH (minimum fat content 35%) also known as pure cream and pouring cream; has no additives like commercially thickened cream.

SOUR (minimum fat content 35%) a thick, commercially-cultured soured cream; good for dips, toppings and baked cheesecakes.

Eggplant also known as aubergine.

Eggs some recipes in this book call for raw or barely cooked eggs; exercise caution if there is a salmonella problem in your area.

Fish we have used raw fish in a few of these recipes. Please check local regulations regarding preparation of raw fish in your community before eating.

Fish sauce also called nam pla or nuoc nam; made from pulverised, salted, fermented, small fish, often anchovies. Has a pungent smell and strong taste; use sparingly. There are many kinds, of varying intensity.

Five-spice powder fragrant mix of ground cinnamon, cloves, star anise, Sichuan pepper and fennel seeds.

Focaccia flat Italian bread.

Galangal also known as laos; a dried root that is a member of the ginger family, used whole or ground, having a piquant, peppery flavour.

Gherkin sometimes known as cornichon; young, dark-green cucumbers grown for pickling.

Ginger
FRESH also known as green or root ginger; the thick gnarled root of a tropical plant. Can be kept, peeled, covered with dry sherry and refrigerated, or frozen in airtight container.

GROUND also known as powdered ginger; used as a flavouring in cakes, pies and puddings, but cannot be substituted for fresh ginger.

PICKLED PINK available from Asian specialty stores; pickled paper-thin shavings of ginger in a mixture of vinegar, sugar and natural colouring.

Gow gee pastry substitute wonton wrappers, spring roll or egg pastry sheets.

Hazelnuts also known as filberts; plump, grape-size, rich, sweet nut having a brown inedible skin that is removed by rubbing heated nuts together vigorously in a tea towel.

baby octopus

calamari rings

scallops

Hoisin sauce a thick, sweet and spicy Chinese paste made from salted fermented soy beans, onions and garlic; used as a marinade or baste, or to accent stir-fries and barbecued or roasted foods.

Horseradish cream prepared paste of grated horseradish, vinegar, oil and sugar.

Kaffir lime leaves aromatic leaves of a citrus tree bearing wrinkle-skinned yellow-green fruit originally grown in South Africa and South-East Asia. Used fresh or dried in many Asian dishes.

Kalonji also known as black onion seeds or nigella.

Ketjap manis Indonesian sweet, thick soy sauce which has sugar and spices added.

Kumara Polynesian name of orange-fleshed sweet potato, often confused with yam.

Lavash flat, unleavened Mediterranean bread.

Lemon grass a tall, lemon-smelling and tasting, sharp-edged grass; the white part of each stem is chopped and used in Asian cooking.

Mirin a sweet, low-alcohol rice wine used in Japanese cooking; sometimes referred to simply as rice wine but should not be confused with sake, the Japanese rice wine made for drinking.

Mixed spice a blend of ground sweet spices including cinnamon, cloves, nutmeg and ginger, occasionally coriander or allspice.

Moroccan spice mix also known as baharat; commercial mixtures can include ground black pepper, cinnamon, cloves, coriander, cumin, nutmeg, paprika, rosemary and turmeric.

Mustard
DIJON a pale brown, distinctively-flavoured, fairly mild French mustard.

SEEDED also known as wholegrain. A French-style coarse-grained mustard made from crushed mustard seeds and Dijon-style French mustard. Seeds can be black or yellow.

Nashi also called Japanese or Asian pear; a member of the pear family but similar in appearance to an apple.

Noodles
BEAN THREAD also called cellophane; made from green mung bean flour. Good softened in soups and salads or deep-fried with vegetables.

DRIED WHEAT may be flat ribbons or thin strands, but they are always long, for they symbolise a long life.

FRESH EGG made from wheat flour and eggs; strands vary in thickness.

FRIED CRISPY EGG packaged (commonly a 100g packet) already deep-fried.

mussels

clams

pipis

2-MINUTE beef flavour quick-cook noodles with flavour sachet.

HOKKIEN also known as stir-fry noodles; fresh wheat flour noodles resembling thick, yellow-brown spaghetti, needing no pre-cooking before being used.

RICE VERMICELLI also known as rice-flour noodles; made from ground rice. Sold dried, are best either deep-fried or soaked then stir-fried, or used in soups.

SOBA Japanese dried noodles made of buckwheat flour.

Nori a type of dried seaweed used in Japanese cooking as a flavouring, garnish or for sushi. Sold in thin sheets, toasted or plain.

Oil

MUSTARD-SEED a mild-tasting oil made from the first pressing of fine yellow mustard seeds; macadamia or hazelnut oil could be used instead.

OLIVE, EXTRA VIRGIN AND VIRGIN the highest quality olive oils, obtained from the first pressings of the olives.

OLIVE a mono-unsaturated oil made from the pressing of tree-ripened olives. Especially good for everyday cooking and as an ingredient. Extra Light or Light describes the mild flavour, not the fat levels.

Pagnotta dry, crusty Italian bread, often herb-flavoured.

Palm sugar very fine sugar from the coconut palm. It is sold in cakes, also known as gula jawa, gula melaka and jaggery. Brown or black sugar can be used as a substitute.

Pancetta an Italian salt-cured pork roll, usually cut from the belly; used, chopped, in cooked dishes to add flavours. Bacon can be substituted.

Paprika ground dried red capsicum (bell pepper), available sweet or hot.

Parsley, flat-leaf also known as continental parsley or Italian parsley.

Pasta

ANGEL HAIR also known as capelli d'angelo; extremely thin dried wheat pasta.

BUCKWHEAT PASTA made from buckwheat flour; Japanese variety is known as soba.

FARFALLE also called butterfly or bow-tie pasta; available fresh and dried.

RISONI small, rice-shaped pasta.

Pawpaw also known as papaya or papaw; large, pear-shaped red-orange tropical fruit. Sometimes used unripe (green) in cooking.

Pesto an Italian paste or thick uncooked sauce, traditionally made with basil, garlic, cheese, oil and pine nuts, and served with pasta or soup. Bottled versions are available in supermarkets. Once opened, keep under refrigeration.

Pide (Turkish bread) comes in long, flat loaves as well as individual rounds; made from wheat flour and sprinkled with sesame or black onion seeds.

Pitta (Lebanese bread) also spelled pita, this wheat-flour pocket bread is sold in large, flat pieces that separate into two paper-thin rounds. Also available in small thick pieces called Pocket Pitta.

Potato, baby (chat) tiny new potato.

Prawns also known as shrimp.

Preserved lemons a North African specialty; lemons are quartered and preserved in salt and lemon juice. To use, remove and discard pulp, squeeze juice from rind, rinse rind well; slice thinly. Serve as part of a mezze or use to add flavour to casseroles or tagines. Sold in jars or singly by delicatessens; once opened, store under refrigeration.

Prosciutto salted-cured, air-dried (unsmoked), pressed ham; usually sold in paper-thin slices, ready to eat.

Pumpkin

BUTTERNUT pear-shaped with golden skin and orange flesh.

Purslane a leafy green that grows wild around the Mediterranean and elsewhere; commonly called pigweed. May be hard to find in shops; substitute baby rocket leaves.

Rice

ARBORIO small, round-grain rice well-suited to absorb a large amount of liquid; especially suitable for use in risottos.

BASMATI a white, fragrant long-grain rice. It should be washed several times before cooking.

BROWN natural whole grain.

CALROSE a medium-grain rice that is extremely versatile; can substitute for short- or long-grain rices if necessary.

KOSHIHIKARI a small, fairly round-grain white rice, developed in Australia for Japanese cooking; ideal for sushi. If unavailable, use white short-grain rice and cook by the absorption method.

Rice paper mostly from Vietnam (banh trang). Made from rice paste and stamped into rounds or squares, with a woven pattern. Stores well at room temperature, although is quite brittle and will break if dropped. Dipped momentarily in water, the sheets become pliable wrappers for fried food and for eating fresh (uncooked) vegetables.

Rigani a type of oregano which grows wild in the mountains of Greece; sold dried, it has a sharp, strong flavour. Substitute fresh or dried oregano or marjoram.

Saffron stigma of a member of the crocus family, available in strands or ground form; imparts a yellow-orange colour to food once infused. Quality varies greatly; the best is the most expensive spice in the world. Should be stored in the freezer.

Sake Japan's favourite rice wine is used in cooking, marinating and as part of dipping sauces. If sake is unavailable, dry sherry, vermouth or brandy can be used as a substitute. When consumed as a drink, it is served warm; to do this, stand the container in hot water for about 20 minutes to warm the sake.

Salsa, bottled is a combination of tomatoes, onions, capsicums, vinegar, herbs and spices.

Sambal oelek (also ulek or olek) Indonesian in origin; a salty paste made from ground chillies.

rice vermicelli

soba

2-minute noodles

thick egg noodles

rice-stick noodles

bean thread noodles

hokkien noodles

rice noodles

thin egg noodles

scampi

prawn

Scampi Italian name for the sweet-tasting seawater shellfish that look like giant prawns; they're also called langoustines and Dublin Bay prawns. Local supplies are caught off the Western Australian coast.

Seasoned pepper a packaged preparation of combined black pepper, red capsicum (bell pepper), paprika and garlic.

Seeds
CUMIN also known as zeera.
CORIANDER widely used in Asian and North African cooking, the seeds have a much more aromatic, lemony flavour than ground coriander.
POMEGRANATE also called anardana; dried and ground, they lend an acidic piquancy to a variety of dishes.
SESAME Black and white are the most common of the oval seeds harvested from the tropical plant *Sesamum indicum*; however there are red and brown varieties also. Used in za'atar, halva and tahini and a good source of calcium. To toast, spread seeds evenly on oven tray, briefly toast in moderate oven.
WHITE POPPY also known as kas kas; quite dissimilar to the black poppy seeds familiar to Western cooks, these seeds from the white poppy are used, ground, as a thickening agent in sauces or as a substitute for ground almonds.

Snow peas also called mange tout ("eat all").

Soy sauce made from fermented soy beans. Several variations are available in most supermarkets and Asian food stores.

Spinach, English correct name for spinach; the green vegetable often called spinach is correctly known as Swiss chard, silverbeet or seakale. Delicate, crinkled green leaves on thin stems; high in iron, it's good eaten raw in salads or steamed gently on its own.

Stock 1 cup (250ml) stock is the equivalent of 1 cup (250ml) water plus 1 crumbled stock cube (or 1 teaspoon stock powder).

Sugar we used coarse, granulated table sugar, also known as crystal sugar, unless otherwise specified.
BROWN an extremely soft, finely granulated sugar retaining molasses for its characteristic colour and flavour.

Tabasco sauce brand name of an extremely fiery sauce made from vinegar, hot red peppers and salt.

Tahini a rich, buttery paste made from crushed sesame seeds; used in making hummus and other Middle-Eastern sauces.

Tamarind the reddish-brown pulp, stones, rind and roots of the bean of the tamarind tree. To extract its acidic, sour essence, soak in boiling water until cool then press though a sieve back into the soaking water; use the flavoured water and discard the pulp.
PULP the dehydrated meat of the tamarind tree's pods; reconstitute by soaking in a small amount of hot water then pressing through a sieve back into the soaking water. Use the liquid and discard the pulp.
THICK CONCENTRATE a thick, purple-black, ready-to-use paste extracted from the pulp of the tamarind bean; used in sauces and casseroles.

Tofu also known as bean curd, an off-white, custard-like product made from the "milk" of crushed soy beans; comes fresh as soft or firm, and processed as fried or pressed dried sheets. Leftover fresh tofu can be refrigerated in water (which is changed daily) up to four days. Silken tofu refers to the method by which it is made – where it is strained through silk.

Tortillas thin, round unleavened bread originating in Mexico; can be made at home or purchased frozen, fresh or vacuum-packed. Two kinds are available, one made from wheat flour and the other from corn (maizemeal).

Vinegar
BALSAMIC authentic only from the province of Modena, Italy; made from a regional wine of white Trebbiano grapes specially processed then aged in antique wooden casks to give the exquisite and pungent flavour.
CHAMPAGNE made from Champagne by a slow process which encourages the distinctive flavour.
CIDER made from fermented apples.
RASPBERRY made from fresh raspberries steeped in a white wine vinegar.
RICE WINE made from fermented rice.
WHITE made from spirit of cane sugar.
WHITE WINE made from white wine.

Wakame a dried seaweed used in Japanese cooking; dark greenish-black and extremely rich in calcium, it can be shredded for salads, reconstituted in hot water and eaten as a vegetable or simmered in soups. Available from Japanese and some other Asian food shops; you can use any edible dried seaweed or kelp in its place.

Wasabi an Asian horseradish used to make a fiery sauce traditionally served with Japanese raw fish dishes.

Wonton wrappers gow gee, egg or spring roll pastry sheets can be substituted.

Yabbies Australian freshwater crayfish; brown to olive or blue-green in colour, they turn orange-red when cooked. Available through fresh fish outlets.

Yogurt plain, unflavoured yogurt, in addition to being good eaten on its own, can be used as a meat tenderiser, as the basis for various sauces and dips or as an enricher and thickener.

Zucchini flowers also called squash flowers; the soft, yellow flowers, available in specialist greengrocers from spring through summer, are a popular Italian first course when filled with a savoury stuffing and baked or dipped in batter and fried.

WARNING
Some dressings in this book contain uncooked eggs; we recommend that you avoid these recipes if there is a salmonella problem where you live.

DEEP-FRYING ADDS FAT
As a general rule, if a recipe calls for deep-frying, add an extra 10g to 15g of fat per serve to the fat count, depending on the surface area of the food.

index

facts and figures

Wherever you live, you'll be able to use our recipes with the help of these easy-to-follow conversions. While these conversions are approximate only, the difference between an exact and the approximate conversion of various liquid and dry measures is but minimal and will not affect your cooking results.

dry measures

metric	imperial
15g	1/2oz
30g	1oz
60g	2oz
90g	3oz
125g	4oz (1/4lb)
155g	5oz
185g	6oz
220g	7oz
250g	8oz (1/2lb)
280g	9oz
315g	10oz
345g	11oz
375g	12oz (3/4lb)
410g	13oz
440g	14oz
470g	15oz
500g	16oz (1lb)
750g	24oz (1 1/2lb)
1kg	32oz (2lb)

liquid measures

metric	imperial
30ml	1 fluid oz
60ml	2 fluid oz
100ml	3 fluid oz
125ml	4 fluid oz
150ml	5 fluid oz (1/4 pint/1 gill)
190ml	6 fluid oz
250ml	8 fluid oz
300ml	10 fluid oz (1/2 pint)
500ml	16 fluid oz
600ml	20 fluid oz (1 pint)
1000ml (1 litre)	1 3/4 pints

helpful measures

metric	imperial
3mm	1/8in
6mm	1/4in
1cm	1/2in
2cm	3/4in
2.5cm	1in
5cm	2in
6cm	2 1/2in
8cm	3in
10cm	4in
13cm	5in
15cm	6in
18cm	7in
20cm	8in
23cm	9in
25cm	10in
28cm	11in
30cm	12in (1ft)

helpful measures

The difference between one country's measuring cups and another's is, at most, within a 2 or 3 teaspoon variance. (For the record, 1 Australian metric measuring cup holds approximately 250ml.) The most accurate way of measuring dry ingredients is to weigh them. When measuring liquids, use a clear glass or plastic jug with the metric markings. (One Australian metric tablespoon holds 20ml; one Australian metric teaspoon holds 5ml.)

If you would like to purchase *The Australian Women's Weekly* Test Kitchen's metric measuring cups and spoons (as approved by Standards Australia), turn to page 120 for details and order coupon. You will receive:
- a graduated set of 4 cups for measuring dry ingredients, with sizes marked on the cups.
- a graduated set of 4 spoons for measuring dry and liquid ingredients, with amounts marked on the spoons.

Note: North America, NZ and the UK use 15ml tablespoons. All cup and spoon measurements are level.

We use large eggs having an average weight of 60g.

oven temperatures

These oven temperatures are only a guide. Always check the manufacturer's manual.

	C° (Celsius)	F° (Fahrenheit)	Gas Mark
Very slow	120	250	1
Slow	150	300	2
Moderately slow	160	325	3
Moderate	180 - 190	350 - 375	4
Moderately hot	200 - 210	400 - 425	5
Hot	220 - 230	450 - 475	6
Very hot	240 - 250	500 - 525	7

how to measure

When using graduated metric measuring cups, shake dry ingredients loosely into the appropriate cup. Do not tap the cup on a bench or tightly pack the ingredients unless directed to do so. Level top of measuring cups and measuring spoons with a knife. When measuring liquids, place a clear glass or plastic jug with metric markings on a flat surface to check accuracy at eye level.

Looking after your interest...

Keep your Home Library cookbooks clean, tidy and within easy reach with slipcovers designed to hold up to 12 books. *Plus* you can follow our recipes perfectly with a set of accurate measuring cups and spoons, as used by *The Australian Women's Weekly* Test Kitchen.

TO ORDER

Mail or fax Photocopy or complete the coupon below and post to AWW Home Library Reader Offer, ACP Direct, PO Box 7036, Sydney NSW 1028, *or* fax to (02) 9267 4363.

Credit cards Have your details ready then, if you live in Sydney, phone 9260 0000; if you live elsewhere in Australia, phone 1800 252 515 (free call, Mon-Fri, 8.30am-5.30pm).

PRICE

Book Holder $11.95 (Australia); elsewhere $A21.95.

Metric Measuring Set $5.95 (Australia); $A8.00 (New Zealand); $A9.95 elsewhere. Prices include postage and handling. This offer is available in all countries.

PAYMENT

Australian residents We accept the credit cards listed on the coupon, money orders and cheques.

Overseas residents We accept the credit cards listed on the coupon, drafts in $A drawn on an Australian bank, and also British, New Zealand and U.S. cheques in the currency of the country of issue. Credit card charges are at the exchange rate current at the time of payment.

- -

✂

☐ **BOOK HOLDER**   ☐ **METRIC MEASURING SET**

Please indicate number(s) required.

Mr/Mrs/Ms _____

Address _____

_____

Postcode _____ Country _____

Ph: Bus. Hours:(   ) _____

I enclose my cheque/money order for $_____ payable to ACP Direct

OR: please charge my

☐ Bankcard ☐ Visa ☐ MasterCard ☐ Diners Club ☐ Amex

Expiry Date ____/____

Cardholder's signature_____

Please allow up to 30 days for delivery within Australia. Allow up to 6 weeks for overseas deliveries. Both offers expire 31/05/00.
HLSALC99